THE PARADOX OF FREEDOM

Owing to the antiquity and rarity of this book, certain pages are regrettably absent, and readability is compromised due to the blurring of the original text. If you possess any insights regarding the availability of these missing sections, kindly inform us. Your assistance is crucial in ensuring the completion of this significant work for the benefit of future generations.

THE PARADOX OF FREEDOM

DHIRENDRANATH SEN

GYAN

Published by

GYAN

Gyan Publishing House
5, Ansari Road
Daryaganj, New Delhi-110002
Phone: 011-47034999, 9811692060
E-mail: books@gyanbooks.com

Distribution Network
gyanbooks.com
India, USA, Canada, UK, Australia

ISBN: 978-93-7447-699-4 (PB)

2nd Impression 2026

Printed at: Gyan Press, Delhi.

THE PARADOX OF FREEDOM
Author: DHIRENDRANATH SEN

THE PARADOX OF FREEDOM

THE PARADOX
of
FREEDOM

Dhirendranath Sen, M.A., Ph.D.,

Lecturer in Constitutional and Administrative, Law, Public Administration and Journalism, University College of Arts, Calcutta, Ex-Editor, Hindusthan Standard and Advance; and lately Member, Editorial Board, Amrita Bazar Patrika

VIDYODAYA LIBRARY PRIVATE LIMITED

72 MAHATMA GANDHI ROAD :: CALCUTTA 9

PREFACE

The Paradox of Freedom embodies the author's reflections on the happenings in India since the publication, in 1954, of his book *From Raj to Swaraj.* Naturally they have reference to the constitutional changes, the trends in our domestic and foreign policy and the country's exact position within the community of nations known as the Commonwealth and Empire and without, which these eventful years have witnessed. On each of these topics not only is there a good deal of controversy but, what is more disquieting, confusion of thinking seems to govern policy among the 'Left' no less than among the 'Right'. There is, however, a difference. The 'Right' deliberately create confusion by stealing the 'Left' thunder, whereas the 'Left' add to it by playing around and apparently cultivating what in Marxian terminology passes for 'Right' deviations. An attempt is made in these pages to place the entire picture in perspective and throw some light, as far as possible, where light is most needed.

The idea canvassed in these pages is dealt with in three Parts. Part I is an examination of the constitutional amendments effected during the last five or six years with a view to their correct assessment. In Part II an analysis is made of India's social developments as viewed from the Marxian angle in the context of the recent trends in Soviet-thinking and the Indian Communist Party's interesting, if rather dubious, experiment with Parliamentary democracy of the British-type both as a Government in the State of Kerala and in the role of the Opposition in some of the other States and at the Centre. Part III seeks to give a bird's eye view of the gradual evolution of a vast Colonial Empire into a Commonwealth of sovereign States with the British Monarch as the Head of that 'freely associated' partnership, of the historic processes that have led to that evolution and of the compelling considerations that have weighed with the Congress leadership in making India a shareholder of that partnership.

We constantly remind ourselves of our 'hard-won freedom'. That seems to suggest that we try to feel the sensation of freedom because we have our own doubts as to where exactly we are and what we are about. Freedom does not drop from the blue heavens or come, all of a sudden, as a gift, maybe, reluctant but, by the motion of the capitalist law, obligatory gift. Such a gift tends to immobilise the revolutionary energy of a people's liberation movement and to foster illusions. It is open to controversy as to whether freedom with an Imperialist Government's sanction is freedom adequately and effectively earned and ensured. The whole Indo-British transaction in the shape of transfer of power seems to unfold the story of an exhausted but opportunist leadership's negotiating, across the counter, a heavy bill of goods and letting the Commonwealth hooks into a dismembered India's none-too-plentiful dough. In the result our freedom is yet no more than a paradox.

It is shocking to think that we are, legally, a free people without freedom in its material or spiritual sense, in the sense, that is, of the continuous and uninterrupted operation of a broad-based liberating process. But an ancient people immersed in prejudice, superstition and the 'other-wordly' inhibitions must be shaken out of their self-complacency. In attempting that task care has been taken, wherever necessary, to cite authoritative documents in support of the contentions urged in these pages. Those documents lend countenance neither to the pretensions of the 'Right' nor to the lucubrations of the 'Left'. This book is, more or less, in the nature of a companion volume to the author's *From Raj to Swaraj* and both the books, it is humbly suggested, should be read together.

Calcutta University,
1st May, 1958

Dhirendranath Sen

CONTENTS

PART I

The Paradox of Freedom

Constitutional Amendments : Deepening Crisis

Since the inauguration of the Indian Republic on January 26, 1950, events of far-reaching political and social significance have taken place throughout the world. These events, in a sense, are reflected at present, rather in a vague way, in the Indian scene as part of the world drama. How and to what extent they may take concrete shape to our benefit will depend on the capacity of our people and Government to react to them in an energetic and conscious manner. The period from August 1947 to January 1950, so far as India is concerned, was one of transition, a period of national self-exaltation darkened by strains and shocks due in part to our political inexperience and immaturity and in part to the aftermath of a terrific event for which we as a people had not been psychologically prepared.

In their own interests no less than in those of the party to whom they handed over power, the British volunteered to train us in the art of 'democratic way' of life and offered the services of a British Governor-General, Lord Mountbatten, to preside over the destiny of the newly created 'Independent Dominion' and produced through Parliament a Dominion version of the Government of India Act, 1935. Apart from the deed of partition, which had been primarily designed adroitly to place the British in a position of strategic vantage *vis-a-vis* the Indian subcontinent and, for that matter, the entire South-East Asia region, the State of Jammu and Kashmir was deliberately left as a pestering sore which threatens to poison the blood of the body politic of this country as well as that of its Pakistani counterpart. It must, however, be admitted to the credit of the British Government that, by withdrawal of their sanction otherwise known as the Crown's paramountcy from the decadent Princely States in response to the inexorable law of social development, they enabled Indian and Pakistani leaders to tackle the Princes successfully and bring the States within the broad political system contemplated in the deed of transfer of power. In short, the British Government put both India and Pakistan on their feet and set the 'democratic' machine in motion.

An Ingenious Formula

Not completely forgetful of the solemn Lahore pledge of complete independence in 1929-30, Congress leaders were naturally perturbed by the thought that Dominion status, whatever the name of its post-war model, would not be accepted as good legal tender by the Indian masses or intellectuals. Consequently, they desperately sought for a formula which would reconcile the vague aspirations of the masses with the urgent requirements of Indo-British capitalist partnership. That formula was discovered at the Commonwealth Prime Ministers' Conference in London in April, 1949. No official report of the Conference as such was published, but there was enough material to indicate the nature of the formula evolved. "A *communique* issued at the end of the meeting contained a declaration stating that the Government of India had informed the Governments of the Commonwealth of the intention of the Indian people that under the new Constitution which was about to be adopted, India should become a sovereign independent Republic. The Government of India had, however, declared and affirmed India's desire to continue her full membership of the Commonwealth of Nations and her acceptance of the King as the symbol of the free association of its independent member-nations and as such, as Head of the Commonwealth. Governments of the other countries of the Commonwealth, the basis of whose membership of the Commonwealth was not thereby changed, accepted and recognised India's continuing membership".[1]

1 *The Commonwealth Relations Office List 1951 (H. M. S. Office)*, P. 66.

From colonial regime (Hong Kong) to self-Government (Singapore); from self-Government to responsible Government (Malaya); from responsible Government to Dominion status (Australia); from Dominion status to Commonwealth partnership (India); from Commonwealth partnership to complete independence under treaty obligations (Burma)—this has been or is the order of evolution of the component parts, old or new, of what has now come to be known as the Commonwealth and Empire. It shows a remarkable flexibility of the Empire structure revealing, as it does, in all its capitalist contradictions, its strength and its weaknesses, its extraordinary capacity for survival and yet its inevitable trend towards disruption and decay. One hears now and then of the dynamics of the Commonwealth idea, of 'the imponderables', as Mr. Nehru puts it, of the Commonwealth. Once formed out of its capitalist foundation it seeks to exsist by itself and is governed by its own laws. Those laws are, perhaps, Mr. Nehru's fascinating 'imponderables'. Against all this historical and social background the framers of our present Constitution declared in its preamble that India is "A Sovereign Democratic Republic".

India as a Commonwealth Republic

There is no denying that formally, at least, India is a fully sovereign State whose people owe no manner of allegiance, unlike the peoples of the other Dominions, to the British King or Queen. There is no mention of the King or Queen in our Constitution. The old prerogatives of the Crown or of its representative are now exercisable, in terms of our Constitution, by the President and, in certain cases, by the Governors of States.[1] The recognition of the King or Queen as the 'symbolic head' of the Commonwealth, of which India continues to be a member, implies, it is suggested, *status*, and has no reference whatsoever to *functions*. The head of our State is the President, elected by an electoral college in accordance with a procedure set out in the Constitution,[2] and there is thus no doubt that

1. *Articles 72 and 161.* 2. *Articles 52-55.*

our State is a *Republic* in fact as well as in law. As to the majority of the Commonwealth countries which have elected to remain within the old monarchical system, the Queen seems to have acquired a 'split' personality. She has a relationship with individuals comprising each such country as well as a relationship with the country as a collective whole. The individuals, though citizens of their respective countries, come within the broad category of *British subjects* and owe allegiance to the Queen, while as collective entities the concerned countries acknowledge her as the head of the Commonwealth. But in the case of the Republics within the Commonwealth (India and Pakistan) the Queen has relationship only with the States, and not with their citizens. In the first case the relationship is both personal and institutional ; in the second the relationship is, in form, institutional.

That India is politically *sovereign* admits of no doubt, for the power to command, sanction or coerce, that is, the power to frame policy and make and enforce law belongs to it to the exclusion of any other internal or external authority. It is, moreover, not only a sovereign Republic but a *democratic* Republic as well. It is *democratic* because the main formal democratic processes, such as provisions for adult franchise, popular election of representatives in Parliament and in State Legislatures, the responsibility of the executive and what are commonly described as Fundamental Rights, etc., are incorporated in our Constitution. To suggest, as was suggested some years ago by certain political parties with reference to the transfer of power, that the political sovereignty of India was fake, was wrong. Evidently, they ignored (I) the elaborate processes of evolution of the British Empire and its adaptability to changing circumstances ; (II) the legal competence of the relevant Indian authorities to command, sanction and coerce ; (III) the increasing power of the Indian bourgeoisie to bargain and manoeuvre ; and (IV) the historic necessity of the metropolitan capital tending towards decolonisation as a measure of security against the spread of the Communist doctrine. It is equally wrong to think, as the parties referred to above have started thinking for the last two or three years, that India is completely independent in the sense in which the U. S. A. or the U. S. S. R. is independent or in the sense in which the Indian people had contemplated complete independence ever since the Congress official declaration in that regard in 1929-30.

India is a sovereign democratic Republic all right, but she is nonetheless one of the nine or ten (if the Malayan Federation is included in this category) Commonwealth States including Britain at one end and Ghana (formerly the Gold Coast) at the other end. And as a Commonwealth State it has certain commitments and obligations in relation to the member-States and the organisation as a whole, which certainly place it along with the member-States in a political category that is as interesting as it is, in a measure, confusing.

The legal, political and economic implications of Commonwealth membership, which will be dealt with in a separate chapter in some detail, seem to have been completely lost sight of by those parties or individuals, who are disposed to assess India's position and functions in the counsels of nations in terms of certain provisions of the Constitution and the statements made from time to time by Prime Minister Nehru on what is called our foreign policy. This kind of assessment, I am afraid, is rather superficial and fails to give a full and comprehensive picture of the significant role of the Commonwealth and the invisible influence of the institution of the English monarchy in the intra-Commonwealth relations. Further, they do not take account of the varying degrees of economic competence and defence potential of the member-States in the mechanism, which render equality among them to a large extent nugatory.

A Bourgeois Socialistic Pattern

Now, the question is, what is the class character of our Republic ? It is, on the face of it, a democracy in the western sense. Consequently, it is a bourgeois democracy of the British model. But a bourgeois democracy of the western type presupposes a particular phase of capitalist development and definite ideological and cultural patterns. None of these essential pre-requisites seem to be present in our country. As a matter of fact, our ideological and cultural patterns are, on the whole, mainly tribal, feudal and non-secular. The result is a continuous conflict between the democratic and secular professions of the political platform and the tribal, reactionary and anti-democratic practices. It is well known that Prime Minister Nehru misses not a single opportunity to warn his countrymen of the dangers of casteism, communalism, provincialism and, indeed, of all the *isms* of the cult of the dark Middle Ages.

As a bourgeois democracy of the British parliamentary model superimposed upon the bullock-cart, the ubiquitous *charka* and a pathetic faith in magic, our Constitution is, of necessity, subjected to violent periodic jolts. The ruling party has found a way out of this extremely difficult situation in the socialistic pattern of society—a made-easy formula given to the people at the Avadi session of the Congress in 1955. This formula, however, introduces no innovation inasmuch as its germs are there in Part IV of the Constitution, which deals with the *Directive Principles of State Policy* as distinct from the *Fundamental Rights* as incorporated in Part III. If one looks up our Constitution and goes carefully into its provisions, one is led to think that our Constitution-makers proceeded to prepare their document on the basis of the Government of India Act, 1935, and reproduced *mutatis mutandis* its familiar phrases, its turns of expressions and even its punctuation symbols, with a few adaptations from the Constitutions of the U. S. A., the Weimer Republic, Eire and Japan. The document is no better than an amateurish essay by an august body of learned men whose minds had been steeped in the English constitutional lore and whose vision had been confined to the doctrinaire postulates of western democracy which had little or no relevance to the objective conditions of our country.

The socialistic pattern of society is certainly not socialism in the Marxian sense as interpreted and amplified by Lenin.

It seems to imply (I) a mixed economy of public ownership and control side by side with individual enterprise and freedom ; (II) a change in the social structure by and through recognised parliamentary procedures ; (III) repudiation of the class conflict, and the proletarian dictatorship as the transition to socialism ; and (IV) a golden mean through which our freedoms shall broaden from precedent to precedent. In short, it is socialism without a socialist revolution, that is, socialism without socialist content. The idea is to get the best of both the worlds—the world of *socialist dictatorship (?)* and the world of *democratic freedom. (?)*. To this end the ruling party has embarked upon the acquisition of agricultural estates and nationalisation of certain industries and at the same time given guarantees to private capital, both Indian and non-Indian, and associated it with the control and management of nationalised industries and other kinds of public enterprises.

A Copy-Book Text

That our Constitution is a copy-book text borrowed indiscriminately from alien sources is evidenced by the fact that during the last six years the Government of India had to seek Parliament's approval of no less than seven amendments as a desperate attempt to solve problems it had created. It may be argued, as has been argued in certain quarters, that India, like the rest of the world, is in the process of becoming and that, consequently, the country's Constitution must be a dynamic instrument capable of adjusting itself to the growing needs of a developing community. The American precedent is often cited in support of this thesis, although in the context of events there is little or no analogy between our country and the U. S. A. The fact, however, is that from 1787, when the American Federal Union had, for the first time, been established, right up to 1951—a period of about 164 years—the appropriate authorities in the U. S. A. had felt called upon to amend their Constitution on as many as twenty-two occasions. Of these, ten amendments came into operation in 1791, only four years after the framing of the Union's original Constitution. The Thirteenth (1865), Fourteenth (1868), Fifteenth (1870) amendments came in the wake, and as a direct result, of the American Civil War. Even as to the ten amendments of 1791, which constitute what is known as the *Bill of Rights*, it should be noted that they were incorporated as the price of ratification of the original Constitution by the Legislatures of the States. When adopting the Constitution in 1787, it may be recalled, several of the Conventions of the States insisted that certain amendments must be made, and as a result, these ten amendments were finally accepted in 1791. Therefore, the *Bill of Rights*, containing these ten amendments, was in substance, though not *pro forma*, part of the original Constitution. Thus it is clear that in the normal circumstances there have been only nine amendments to the Constitution of the U.S.A., including the latest (1951) laying down, as it does, that no President of the U. S. A. shall be elected to more than two terms, during this long period of 164 years. Of these, again, four amendments [Sixteenth and Seventeenth (1913)], [Eighteenth and Nineteenth (1919)], came in anticipation, or as a result, of World War I. Accordingly, the steps taken in India for the amendments to the Constitution do not bear analogy to the American precedent, either in substance or in the processes through and by which the amendments have been effected.

The Social Implications of Amendments

It does not mean, however, that urgent and important social welfare legislation should be halted on the ground of constitutional handicaps. Where such handicaps stand in the way of the requisite regulatory and prohibitory power being taken by the appropriate authority or authorities in the interest of the community they must be removed as effectively and swiftly as circumstances may permit. But this does not demolish the main complaint canvassed earlier that our Constitution-makers approached the problems confronting them in a mechancial way and in callous disregard of the needs and circumstances of the country and of its teeming millions undermined physically and spiritually, as they had been, over the ages, by hunger, misery and lack of a sense of security and fulfilment. They persuaded themselves that a revised edition of the Government Act, 1935, with a few doctrinaire recitals from the Select Constitutions of the World would do the trick and ensure freedom at home and prestige abroad.

Nor is it correct to hold that all the seven amendments to our Constitution, so far introduced, have been designed to facilitate and promote social welfare legislation. In the Statement of Objects and Reasons of the Bill introduced in Parliament on December 20, 1954, by Prime Minister Nehru, it was observed *inter alia* that "judicial decisions interpreting Articles 14, 19 and 31 have raised serious difficulties in the way of the Union and the States, putting through......social welfare legislation on the desired lines......." The Statement adds : "It is considered therefore necessary to restate more precisely the State's power of compulsory acquisition and requisitioning of private property and distinguish it from cases where the operation of regulatory or prohibitory laws of the State results in the deprivation of private property."

Those observations, it should be noted, had been made with reference to the Fourth Amendment which came into operation in April, 1955. The amendment appeared to have been called for by the decisions of the Supreme Court in *Subodh Gopal Bose's Case*[1] and the Second *Sholapur Mill's Case*[2] and the conflicting opinions expressed by the learned judges. It is true that the decisions of the Supreme Court have, in some important cases, come into conflict with the professed intentions of the State in the matter of social welfare legislation affecting private property. It may be that the learned judges had erred in interpreting the relevant provisions of the Constitution as clearly indicated by the sharp differences of opinion among the judges themselves. It may also be permissible to hold that by training, education and social background judges generally are not sympathetic towards measures calculated to affect or disturb private

1. (1954) S. C. J. 127.
2. (1954) S. C. J. 175.

property notwithstanding the well-known rule of interpretation that courts are governed by the wordings of the Constitution or the Statute, and not by their likes or dislikes in the matter of policies involving social questions. It is none the less undeniable that where the Constitution-makers had chosen to depart from the usual felicitous phraseology of their British predecessors and used their own skill in draftsmanship they showed neither foresight nor awareness of the special significance of the Constitution as distinct from an Act of the Legislature or a piece of ancillary legislation.

Restrictions on Freedoms

That is for the present a different issue. What, however, one must bear in mind in this connection is that there have been cases where the ruling party has sought amendments to the Constitution not for the purposes of social welfare legislation but for curtailing the freedoms as guaranteed in the Constitution, and strengthening the Centre *vis-a-vis* the States. Take, for instance, the First Amendment which came into force on June 18, 1951. Of course, it incorporated a saving for laws providing for the acquisition of estates and validated several Acts and Regulations abridging or taking away certain rights relating to estates.[1] But the Government and their spokesmen are discreetly silent on the drastic changes in the provisions of Article 19 of the Constitution, which seeks to protect the Right to Freedom.

It may be recalled that in 1950, the Supreme Court had given significant rulings on the constitutional guarantee as to freedom of speech and expression as incorporated in Article 19 (I) (a) in *Brij Bhuson* V. *The State of Delhi* and in *Romesh Thapper* V. *The State of Madras.* The Court had held *inter alia* that the freedom of speech and expression could not be curtailed on the plea of prejudicial activity unless it tended to undermine the security of the State or overthrow it, and that public disorder of a minor or local nature could not be construed as undermining or overthrowing the State. In the wake of these decisions came legisla-

1. *Articles 31 A.*

tion at the instance of the Government of India by way of amendment to Article 19 (2), which had retrospective effect.

Thus the rulings of the Supreme Court came to be nullified and the constitutional guarantee as to freedom of speech and expression was brought within the mischief of the entire Panal Code and special or local laws. The only consolation is that the restrictions must be 'reasonable' and that it is open to the competent Courts to decide finally and conclusively what restrictions are 'reasonable' and what restrictions are 'not reasonable'. If any law imposed or sought to impose restrictions on the freedom of speech and expression which were not, in the opinion of the Courts, reasonable, that law could be declared invalid and inoperative to the extent it contained 'unreasonable' restrictions. Incidentally, so far as the State of Jammu and Kashmir is concerned, the 'the reasonable restrictions' shall be construed as meaning such restrictions as the State Legislature deems reasonable, so that even the Supreme Court shall have no jurisdiction in this matter. The other changes contemplated in the First Amendment are, more or less, formal, and not substantial.

The Second Amendment, which came into operation on May 1, 1953, deleted certain words and figures in Article 81 regarding the ratio of representation in the *Lok Sabha* (House of the People) to the size of population in a particular territorial constituency. There is not much of social significance in this amendment. The original Articles 81 and 82 have since been replaced by the present Article 81 in consequence of the changes brought about by the Seventh Amendment which will be discussed later. The present Article 82 is also a product of that amendment, and it provides for readjustment of seats in the *Lok Sabha* and of the territorial constituencies of each State upon the completion of each census.

By the Third Amendment made operative since February 22, 1955, the concurrent jurisdiction of the Union Parliament has been extended to the trade and commerce in, and the production, supply and distribution of, (1) foodstuffs, including edible oil seeds and oils ; (II) cattle fodder, including oilcakes and other concentrates; (3) raw cotton, whether ginned or unginned, and cotton seed; and (IV) raw jute. The same concurrent jurisdiction applies to the imported goods where the control of such goods by the Centre is declared by Parliament to be expedient in public interest. Until this amendment these were subjects of exclusive legislation by the States in so far as they fell under the category of trade and commerce within the States.[1] But now both Parliament and the Legislatures of States have power to legislate in respect of these subjects. And if any provision of a law made by a State Legislature is repugnant to any provision of law made by Parliament with respect to any of the aforesaid matters, then the law made by Parliament shall prevail and that made by a State Legislature shall, to the extent of the repugnancy, be void.[2] Here, then, is an instance in which the Centre has sought, by constitutional changes, extension of its enormous powers, thereby undermining the autonomy of the States in matters of vital concern to them.

Three Categories of Sovereign Power

The Fourth Amendment given effect since April 27, 1955, mainly affects private property and the rights accruing therefrom. It seeks to remove the confusion which was caused by the conflicting opinions expressed by the judges of the Supreme Court on Articles 19 and 31 in *Subodh Gopal Bose's Case* already cited. The learned judges, of course, came to the same conclusion, but three separate judgements were delivered. The broad constitutional issue involved, apart from the merits of the case, was whether it came within the scope of Article 19 (1) (f) or whether it attracted the operation of Article 31. The Chief Justice maintained that Article 31 applied, and with him concurred Mahajan J., and Ghulam Hassan J. On the other hand, S. R. Das J., and Jagannadha Das J. held a different view.

According to Sastri C. J. (now retired), Article 19 (1) enumerates certain freedoms under caption 'Right to

1. *Entry 26 of List 11 and entry 33 of List 111 of the Seventh Schedule.*
2. *Article 254.*

Freedom', and in so far as it relates to property it only declares the citizen's right to own property, and has no reference to the right to the property owned by him, which is dealt with in Article 31. The purpose of the latter is, however, not to declare the right of the State to deprive a citizen of his property but, as the heading of the Article shows, to protect 'the right to property' of every citizen. The Article protects it by defining the limitations on the power of the State to take away private property without the consent of the owner. The first important limitation on that power is that a legislative enactment, as distinct from executive action, is a pre-requisite for its exercise. This limitation is embodied in clause (1) of the Article. Clause (2) imposes two further limitations. The Legislature is prohibited, for instance, from making a law authorising compulsory acquisition or requisitioning of property except (a) for a public purpose and (b) on payment of compensation for the injury sustained by the owner. Clauses (1) and (2) of Article 31 are thus not mutually exclusive in scope and content, but should be read together and understood as dealing with the same subject.

In the opinion of the Chief Justice, the power of *Eminent Domain*, which is assumed to be inherent in the sovereignty of a State according to the Continental and American jurists but which is not expressly provided for in the American Constitutions, is made the subject of an express grant in our Constitution. But the American doctrine of *Police Power*, as a distinct and specific legislative power, is not recognised in our Constitution. It is, accordingly, contrary to the scheme of the Constitution to hold that clause (1) of Article 31 must be read in positive terms and understood as conferring *Police Power* on the Legislature in relation to rights of property. The Chief Justice then proceeds to lay down a thesis, namely, that "social welfare is not inconsistent with the ownership of private property and does not demand arbitrary expropriation of such property by the State without compensation." That, of course, is an *obiter*.

Mr. Justice S. R. Das (now Chief Justice) counters the Chief Justice's interpretation of Articles 19 and 31. In doing so, the learned judge proceeds on the footing that Article 19 relates to abstract right as well as to the right to concrete property. If a citizen loses his property by reason of its having been compulsorily acquired under Article 31, he loses the right to hold that property and cannot complain that his fundamental right under sub-clause (f) of clause (1) of Article 19 has been infringed. Clause (1) of Article 31 deals with deprivation of property in exercise of *Police Power* and enunciates the restriction on the exercise of that power. The restriction means only that if *Police Power* is to be exercised in the matter of deprivation of property, then recourse must be had to a legislative enactment, and not to an executive fiat. Clause (2) of Article 31, on the other hand, deals with the exercise of the Power of *Eminent Domain.* The limitations to which the exercise of such power is subject are: (a) that recourse must be had to a legal enactment; (b) that the power must be exercised for a public purpose; and (c) that provision must be made for compensation.

The exercise of *Police Power* in relation to property may conceivably result, in certain circumstances, in the extinction or destruction of the property in question or in the State's taking the property in its control without involving the transfer of title to itself. In such a case, there is no acquisition of the property by the State, calling for compensation, as under the exercise of *Eminent Domain.*

On the authority of jurists, the learned judge classifies the State's sovereign power into three categories, namely, (a) the *Power of Taxation,* (b) the power of *Eminent Domain,* and (c) the *Police Power.* These, according to him, are distinct categories of sovereign power with different connotations subserving the different needs of the State and society.

It appears from the provisions of the Fourth Amendment[1] and the arguments advanced by the Government in support that the measure is intended to cancel, by legislation, the opinions expressed by the Chief Justice and the two concu-

1. S. 2.

wring judges. A distinction has been made in the amendment between the State's exercise of its power of compulsory acquisition and requisitioning of private property, on the one hand, and the exercise of its power which may result in deprivation of property, on the other. The former is the exercise of *Eminent Domain* which calls for payment of compensation, whereas the latter is exercise of *Police Power* which imposes no such liability on the State. The *Police Power* is exercised in the interest of the community, whereas the power of *Eminent Domain* is exercised to implement a public purpose. The primary purpose of *Police Power* is protective or preventive ; by contrast the power of *Eminent Domain* is constructive and socially ameliorative. In either case, however, action, if any, must be taken on the authority of law, that is, on the authority of an Act of the Legislature. A like legislative protection is given in the matter of taxation.[1] With regard to all the three categories of sovereign power our Constitution has provided for complete protection against the executive organ of the State.

The requirement of provision for payment of compensation, where property is compulsorily acquired or requisitioned, does not mean that compensation shall necessarily be adequate and substantial. It may or may not be so. Whatever compensation the law provides for is perfectly valid, and the law in this regard shall not be called in question in any court on the ground of *inadequacy* of the compensation.[2] Can such law be challenged in a competent court, it may be asked, by reason of the compensation provided for being *unfair and inequitable* as distinguished from its being *inadequate* ? Here, again, there is a lacuna in the amendment which may be exploited by enterprising property-owners through litigation.

Where a law does not provide for the transfer of the ownership or right to possession of any property to the State or to a Corporation owned or controlled by the State, it shall not be construed, in terms of the amendment as having

1. *Article 265.*
2. *Article 31 (2).*

provided for the compulsory acquisition or requisitioning of property, even if it results in depriving any person of his property.[1]

The changes comtemplated in the next section[2] of the amendment extend the scope of Article 31-A, so as to cover certain categories of essential welfare legislation, such as (I) fixing of a ceiling on agricultural holdings, distribution of excess lands, etc. ; (II) utilisation of vacant and waste lands ; (III) full control over the oil and mineral resources ; (IV) temporary taking over, under State management, of commercial or industrial undertakings or other property ; and (V) progressive elimination of the managing agency system, compulsory amalgamation of two or more companies, transfer of an undertaking from one company to another. As a corollary to the above changes, section 5 of the amendment accords retrospective validation of certain State and Central Acts and includes them in the Nineth Schedule to the Constitution.[3] The court's jurisdiction in respect of these Acts is, for all practical purposes, ousted.

The judgement of the Supreme Court in *Saghir Ahmad* V. *The State of U. P.*[4] appeared to have suggested that notwithstanding the competence of the appropriate legislatures to introduce, by legislation, State monopoly in a particular sphere of trade or commerce, the legislation enacted in that behalf might have to be justified before the courts as being in *general public interest*[5] or as not overstepping the limits *of reasonable* restrictions.[6] Section 4 of the amendment is calculated to leave the final decision on the question of *general public interest* or of *reasonable restrictions* to the Legislatures, thereby repelling interference by courts.[7]

The Fifth Amendment, made operative with effect from December 24, 1955, is in the main procedural. It seeks to fill the lacuna in the original Article relating to territorial reorganisation of States.[8] It was required of the President, for instance, by the original Constitution that he would not

---

1. *Article 31 (2A).* 2. *S. 3.* 3. *Article 31-B.*
4. *(1954) S. C. J. 819.* 5. *Articles 301 and 302.* 6. *Article 304 (b).*
7. *Article 305.* 8. *Article 3.*

recommend introduction of a Bill in Parliament for the purposes of territorial reorganisation without ascertaining the views of the Legislatures of the States affected by such reorganisation, but there was no direction in the relevant Article as to the period within which the concerned Legislatures would express their views. By the amendment the President has been empowered to specify the period to be required in this behalf or, if necessary, to extend it.

Encroachments on State Autonomy

The Sixth Amendment, brought into force on September 11, 1956, like the Third Amendment, is a step towards centralisation bringing out in bold relief, as it does, the basic policy of the ruling party pursued consistently since its accession to power in 1947. It deals with the taxing power, and the financial relations between the Centre and the States. Attempts have been, and are being, made to reduce progresssively the units' area of jurisdiction over the sources of revenue. Even the British Government were less hostile to the units than the Congress Government in this respect. It will be seen that the Government of India Act, 1935, had given exclusive power to the Legislatures of the Governor's Provinces in respect of "taxes on the sale of goods and on advertisements."[1] And 'goods' included all materials, commodities and articles,[2] and did not, therefore, exclude newspapers. This power of the Provinces to tax the sale or purchase of newspapers as coming under the general category of 'goods and advertisements' was taken away and made over to the Centre under the original Indian Constitution, 1950.[3]

The States were, however, given authority in respect of taxes over the sale or purchase of goods other than newspapers.[4] Now, by and under the Sixth Amendment[5], apart from the sale or purchase of newspapers, the power of taxation in respect of the sale or purchase of other goods,

1. *26 Geo. 5 ch. 2., entry 48, List II, Seventh Schedule.*
2. *Ibid, S. 311.*
3. *Entry 92, List I, Seventh Schedule.*
4. *Entry 54, List II, Seventh Schedule.* 5. *S. 2.*

which was originally assigned to the States, has been transferred to the Union List, in so far as such sale or purchase takes place in the course of inter-State trade or commerce.[1] Parliament has been empowered to formulate, by legislation, principles for determining when a sale or purchase of goods takes place in the course of inter-State trade or commerce.[2] No longer, it appears, shall the courts be competent to adjudicate on the issue as to whether a particular sale or purchase does or does not form part of inter-State trade or commerce, once the principles in that regard have been laid down by Parliament.

It is, of course, true that in terms of the original Constitution[3] the States had no power to tax the sale or purchase of goods where such sale or purchase took place (a) outside the State, or (b) in course of the import of goods into, or export of the goods out of, the territory of India. But here, again, the amendment lays down that it is Parliament that may decide by legislation, to the exclusion of the courts, when a particular sale or purchase belongs to the one or the other of the two categories mentioned above.[4] Nor is this all. The States' power to tax the sale or purchase thus restricted is further curtailed by the imposition of such restrictions and conditions in regard to the system of levy, rates and other incidents of the tax as Parliament may specify, particularly where the goods concerned are declared by Parliament to be of special importance in inter-State trade or commerce.[5] The restrictions and conditions herein envisaged cannot obviously be challenged in any court of law on the ground of unreasonableness or on any other ground.

Now, an interesting anecdote. A learned French Academician presented himself one day to Cuvier, and said: "I am going to submit to you a question of natural history. Being appointed to correct a part of the letter C in our Dictionary, I have written for the word 'crab'—The crab is a red fish that walks sideways."

---

1. *Entry 92A.* 2. *S. 3.* 3. *Article 286.*
4. *S. 4 (2).* 5. *S. 4 (3).*

"Your definition, Sir", replied Cuvier, "is excellent; by this description all crab-eaters—and they are numerous—will not fail to recognise it."

And calling back the distinguished Academician, Cuvier whispered into his ears: "Between ourselves, the crab is not a fish; it is not red; it does not walk sideways. With these exceptions your definition is perfect; keep it for the benefit of the crab-eaters."

Following Cuvier's ruling on the learned French Academician's definition of 'crab', one may whisper into the ears of our law-givers: "Well, Gentleman, our State is not State; our autonomy is not autonomy; our State autonomy is not State autonomy. With these reservations our State autonomy is complete and perfect."

The Effect of the Reorganisation Act, 1956

I come now to the Seventh and, upto now, last Amendment which has come into force since November 1, 1956. The main effect of this amendment has been the reorganisation of States and the Territories constituting, as they do, what is known as the territory of India. The changes brought about are to the effect: (I) that the original classification of States and Territories into A, B, and C States and D Territory has been done away with; (II) that all the former Princely States with the minor exceptions of Himachal Pradesh in which is incorporated Bilaspur, and Manipur and Tripura have been integrated in the States; (III) that the office of Rajpramukhs as heads of States has been abolished; (IV) that the entire country has been divided into States and Union Territories; (V) that the States have been placed on a footing of equality with one another both in regard to status and functions irrespective of size and population with Governors appointed by the President as heads, except in the case of the State of Jammu and Kashmir which has been accorded preferential treatment; (VI) that the Union Territories have been placed in charge of the President who is required to administer them, acting to such extent as he thinks fit, through an administrator to be appointed by him with such designation as he may specify subject, however, to the proviso that the President may appoint a State Governor as the administrator of an adjoining Union Territory, in which case the Governor shall exercise his functions as such administrator independently of his Council of Ministers ; and (VII) that the Union Territories have been given no powers of legislation, such powers being exercised by Parliament,[1] except in the case of the Union Territory of (a) the Andaman and Nicober Islands ; and (b) the Laccadive, Minicoy and Amindivi Islands, in respect of which the President may make regulations for the peace, progress and good government of such territory.[2] As a corollary, certain consequential changes have been incorporated in the Constitution.

In order to understand the principles underlying the reorganisation of States one should read the Seventh Amendment with the relevant provisions of the States Reorganisation Act, 1956, which preceded it. On the whole, the reorganisation has been effected on the basis of language, keeping in view administrative convenience, viability and, above all, the unitary aims and purposes of pseudo-federal political engineering. Language and culture as determining factors in the scheme of reorganisation have been disregarded in the case of Guzrat and Maharastra and, to a comparatively minor degree, of Punjab. West Bengal has fared rather badly while Orissa's insistent demand for restoration to her of Kharswan and Seraikella has proved a cry in the wilderness in the face of stubborn resistance by Hindi-speaking Bihar. The States as reorganised and Union Territories are as follows :[3]

I. The States

1. Andhra Pradesh. 2. Assam. 3. Bihar. 4. Bombay. 5. Kerala. 6. Madhya Pradesh. 7. Madras. 8. Mysore. 9. Orissa. 10. Punjab. 11. Rajasthan. 12. Uttar Pradesh. 13. West Bengal. 14. Jammu and Kashmir.

II. The Union Territories

1. Delhi. 2. Himachal Pradesh. 3. Manipur. 4. Tripura. 5. The Andaman and Nicober Islands. 6. The Laccadive, Minicoy and Amindivi Islands.

---

1. *Article 246 (4)* 2. *Article 240.*
3. *Articles 1 and 4, and the First Schedule*

The last, it seems, has not yet been said and heard about properly constructed linguistic States with powers of autonomy, far greater and much more extensive than the High Command of the ruling party is prepared at the moment to concede or yield. As a matter of precaution, however, it has set up five Zonal Councils[1] to achieve what has recently been declared by Home Minister Pant, Chairman of these Councils, as "emotional integration." This sort of "a corrective to regional and linguistic loyalties", as distinguished from what I may call the idealistically pre-determined national will, was envisaged in Article 263 of the original Constitution which, of course, is retained in its revised text.

Five Zonal Councils

The Reorganisation Act with its provisions for Zonal Councils marks a step forward towards centralisation which, in effect, is tantamount to a corresponding reduction in the operational autonomy of the States. A Union Minister appointed by the President shall be Chairman of each of these five Zonal Councils. Besides the Chairman, each Council shall consist, amongst others, of the Chief Minister and two other Ministers of each State included in the zone. The functions of the Council shall be advisory. It may discuss and make recommendations with regard to (a) any matter of common interest in the field of economic and social planning ; (b) any matter concerning border disputes, linguistic minorities or inter-State transport ; and (c) any matter connected with, or arising out of, the reorganisation of the States.

So long as the same political party is in office at the Centre and in each of the States included in a zone, there may be no friction. All questions at a meeting of a Zonal Council shall be decided by a majority of the votes of the members and, in the case of a tie, the Chairman shall have a second or casting vote. Each zone may, in such circumstances, tend to develop into an intermediary super-State in the three-tier mechanism with the result that the States will be left with nothing to chew or bite. That seems to be the

1. *The States Reorganisation Act, 1956, Part III.*

design of the grand scheme of Home Minister Pant's 'emotional integration.' If, on the other hand, a different party comes to office in one or more States in a zone, there is bound to be friction in so far as the present ruling party may try to go ahead with its scheme to reduce State autonomy, to all intents and purposes, to a nullity. In any case, there are reasons to suspect that although the proposal to integrate Bihar and West Bengal has been abandoned under mass political pressure, the reconstruction of Bombay as a bi-lingual State and institution of the Zonal Councils are steps which would give cause for disquiet among those who stand for linguistic States.

The five zones have been constituted in the following manner :—

(a) The Northern Zone, comprising the States of Punjab, Rajasthan, Jammu and Kashmir and the Union Territories of Delhi and Himachal Pradesh ; (b) the Central Zone, comprising the States of Uttar Pradesh and Madhya Pradesh ; (c) the Eastern Zone, comprising the States of Bihar, West Bengal, Orissa, and Assam and the Union Territories of Manipur and Tripura ; (d) the Western Zone, comprising the States of Bombay and Mysore ; and (e) the Southern Zone, comprising the States of Andhra Pradesh, Madras and Kerala.

Additional Provisions Relating to Citizenship

It seems pertinent to refer in this connection to the provisions of citizenship made by or under the Citizenship Act, 1955, in addition to those incorporated in the original Constitution of 1950. These, it is clear, have been brought about by the ordinary process of legislation in the exercise of powers implicit in Parliament,[1] and not by recourse to the procedure[2] for amending the Constitution. Consequently, the changes thus introduced are not formally constitutional amendments ; nor, again, are they anything but complementary. They are nevertheless of constitutional significance in so far as they have filled up the gaps of the original Constitution in regard to the question of such great

1. *Article 11.* 2. *Article 368.*

political and social importance. Provision has been made in the Act for the aquisition of citizenship by (I) birth, (II) descent, (III) registration, (IV) naturalisation and (V) incorporation of territory.

Every person born in India on or after January 26, 1950, shall be a citizen *by birth*. The exceptions are where (a) the concerned person's father possesses diplomatic immunity, and is not himself a citizen ; and (b) his father is an enemy alien, and his birth occurs in a place then under the enemy's occupation.[1] A person born outside India on or after January 26, 1950, shall be a citizen *by descent* if his father is a citizen at the time of his birth, subject, again, to certain restrictions.[2]

The appropriate Indian authority empowered in that behalf may *register* as a citizen any person who is not already such a citizen, and belongs to any of the following categories[3] : (a) persons of Indian origin ordinarily resident in India and have been so resident for six months immediately before making application for registration ; (b) persons of Indian origin ordinarily resident in any country or place outside undivided India ; (c) women who are, or have been, married to citizens of India ; (d) minor children of persons who are citizens of India ; and (e) persons of full age and capacity who are citizens of a Commonwealth country. The admission of citizens of a Commonwealth country to Indian citizenship shall be on a reciprocal basis, that is, due regard must be had to the conditions under which Indian citizens may, by law or practice of the Commonwealth country in question, become citizens of that country by registration. No person being of full age shall be registered as a citizen under any of these categories until he has taken the oath of allegiance to the Constitution of the country.[4] A person shall be deemed to be of *Indian origin* if he, or either of his parents, or any of his grand-parents was born in undivided India. Indian citizenship *by registration* is thus thrown open to large sections of people who have hitherto been Stateless, such, for example, as

---

1. S. 3. 2. S. 4. 3. S. 5. 4. S. 5 (3).

certain *migrants* from Pakistan and children of the citizens of India born after the commencement of the Constitution.

If a foreigner (and the expression 'foreigner' does not include a Commonwealth citizen) makes an application for the grant of a certificate of naturalisation, the Central Government may admit such an eligible person to citizenship by naturalisation.[1] For aquisition of such citizenship certain conditions will have to be fulfilled except in the case of eminent persons who have rendered distinguished service to the cause of science, philosophy, art, literature, world peace or human progress generally. To describe Pakistanis admitted to Indian citizenship as *naturalised* citizens is absolutely wrong.

If any territory becomes part of India, the Central Government may specify the persons who shall be India's citizens by reason of their connection with that territory. The latest example of the acquistion of such citizenship (through *incorporation of territory*) is furnished by the people of Chandernagore in West Bengal, which was formerly a French possession and has now been incorporated in the territory of India.

Citizens *Qua* Citizens

Provisions have also been made for the renunciation of Indian citizenship[2] as well as for its termination.[3] Again, the Central Government may, by order, deprive certain persons of Indian citizenship, but this may apply only to (I) citizens by naturalisation ; (II) citizens under clause (c) of Article 5 of the Constitution, that is, persons of Indian domicile who had been ordinarily resident in India for not less than five years immediately preceding the commencement of the Constitution ; and (III) citizens by registration otherwise than under clause (b) (ii) of Article 6 of the Constitution or clause (a) of sub-section (1) of Section 5 of the Citizenship Act. Thus a distinction is made between citizens with reference to the processes by or through which citizenship has been acquired by them. Take an extreme case. The Central Government would perfectly be within

1. *S.* 6. 2. *S.* 8. 3. *S.* 9.

its rights under this provision, should it so desire, to deprive, say, Professor Satish Chandra Ghosh, *Ex*-mayor of Calcutta ; Dr. P. C. Ghosh, *Ex*-Chief Minister of West Bengal ; or Mr. Bhupesh Gupta, M. P., and a leader of the Indian Communist Party, of their citizenship, but it cannot touch or affect the status of Mr. Govind Ballav Pant ; Dr. Radhakrishnan ; or even Mr. Hem Chandra Naskar, West Bengal's Fisheries Minister. And why, it may be asked ? Because, I contend, the first-named three persons are citizens in terms of clause (c) of Article 5 of the Constitution, whereas the other three are citizens by clauses (a) and (b) of the same article. This analysis may, for all practical purposes, be of academic nature, but the illustrations cited above show how absurd and fantastic is the law or the logic of the New Delhi law-givers.

The far-reaching implication of the provision relating to the deprivation of citizenship will be clear from the direction that action in that regard may be taken by the Central Government where it is satisfied that the citizen concerned "has shown himself by act or speech to be disloyal or disaffected towards the Constitution as by law established." Such executive action is, of course, subject to an administrative or quasi-judical enquiry, and the aggrieved party is entitled to defend himself, but the court shall have no power, as far as it appears to me, to interfere. And what, on earth, is the meaning of the expression "disloyal or disaffected towards the Constitution" ? If, for instance, one, rightly or wrongly, says that the Constitution has set up a bourgeois dictatorship and should be thrown out, does one attract the operation of the law ? If it does, nothing could be more dangerously authoritarian and mischievous.

Social and Political Trends

Coming back to the Amendments, a careful examination of their contents reveals the broad social and political pattern of our 'democracy' and some of its characteristic features. First, they are all, more or less, directed towards strengthening the unitary character of the political system and reducing the States, by and large, to the position of the agencies of a centralised bourgeois-cum-bureaucratic dictatorship. And this is being done in the name of national unity or 'emotional integration'—an unedifying specimen of senseless but, on a long view, dangerous chatter. Second, some of them are, and have been, intended to counter the decisions of the highest court of law and reduce drastically its area of jurisdiction. Such a step is bound to undermine people's faith in judicial processes and the sanctity, if any, of the Constitution—a proceeding which is likely to pave the way, in the course of time, to a totalitarian plutocracy. Third, the provisions of one amendment at least have struck a blow at civil liberties, especially the freedom of speech and expression—a desperate measure which seems to have taken us back to the days of the Privy Council's colonial ruling in *Bal Gangadhar Tilak's Case* by setting aside, by legislation, healthy democratic principles laid down by the Federal Court and the Supreme Court in a number of important judgements. Fourth, some of the amendments, it must be admitted, have removed constitutional impediments in the way of social welfare legislation—a welcome step long overdue but which, in the absence of a conscious revolutionary situation, may be utilised to lay the foundations of discredited and reactionary State capitalism or national socialism to canalise the urges and aspirations of the masses and intellectuals in dangerously mystic somnolence. Altogether the amendments and the trends they reveal present an overall picture which is anything but edifying or inspiring.

The Anomolous Position of Jammu and Kashmir

The special treatment accorded to the State of Jammu and Kashmir under the constitutional arrangements earlier referred to in this chapter calls for more than a passing notice. The legal position of the State is rather curious. Under the municipal law of India it is one of the Union's fourteen States. Its territory is the territory which, immediately before the commencement of the Constitution, was comprised in the Indian State of Jammu and Kashmir.[1] As

1. *First Schedule to The Constitution (Seventh Amendment) Act, 1956; Article 1.*

against this, the Pakistani Constitution lays down: "When the people of the State of Jammu and Kashmir decide to accede to Pakistan, the relation between Pakistan and the said State shall be determined in accordance with the wishes of the people of that State".[1] Unlike India Pakistan, of course, does not yet claim that the State of Jammu and Kashmir is an integral part of its territory. The relevant constitutional provision nevertheless assumes two things. It assumes, in the first place, that there has been no accession by it to India or that the accession, if any, is illegal and of no effect. It assumes, in the second place, that its accession to Pakistan is only a question of time. There is no 'if' in this proposition, and when the accession to Pakistan, in fact, takes place, which evidently is taken for granted, the nature and character of the relationhip between Pakistan and the State shall be determined according as the people concerned may decide. On the other hand, Jammu and Kashmir appears, in the eye of the United Nations, to be 'disputed property', having regard to the commitments, made conditionally by India, and without any reservation by Pakistan, that the future of the State shall be finally settled by a democratic plebiscite. *Defacto*, however, Indian sovereignty extends, within the limits of constitutional arrangements between India and the State, to about two-thirds of its territory while the residuary portion is physically under the control of Pakistan.

India *Versus* Pakistan

The situation is confusing and is fraught with dangerous possibilities. For this the Government of India, it must be frankly stated, cannot absolve itself of its share of responsibility. Provisions, it may be recalled, had been made in the Government of India Act, 1935, adapted in terms of the Indian Independence Act, 1947, for accession of the Indian States to India or to Pakistan.[2] The Act laid down *inter alia:* "An Indian State shall be deemed to have acceded to the Dominion if the Governor-General has signified his acceptance of an Instrument of Accession

1. *Article 203.* 2. *S. 6.*

executed by the Ruler thereof etc., etc.,......" Thus two conditions were contemplated for accession. First, the execution of an Instrument of Accession by the Ruler concerned was necessary. It was essential, in the second place, that the relevant Governor-General must signify his acceptance of the Instrument of Accession as executed by the Ruler. Once these two conditions were fulfilled the validity of the accession was not open to question. These provisions had been incorporated in a statute passed by the British Parliament and accepted by both India and Pakistan. It was accordingly not open to any of these three parties—the British Government, the Government of India and the Government of Pakistan—to challenge any Instrument of Accession executed and recognised in terms of the adapted Government of India Act, 1935.

The question was whether or not the accession of the State of Jammu and Kashmir to India was in accordance with the Act. If the answer to that question was in the affirmative, then the State became an integral part of the territory of India and any raid into the State amounted to a raid into Indian territory. There is not the slightest evidence that the conditions for accession referred to above were not fulfilled in the case of the accession of the State to India. Legally, the accession was perfectly in order and valid.

The Pakistani Government's contention, on the contrary, has been or is that when the accession took place, the Maharajah had no authority to execute the Instrument because the people of the State had already taken control of the situation and that, consequently, it was they and not the Maharajah who alone had the right to decide the issue finally and conclusively. One wonders whether Pakistani leaders and their foreign supporters are aware of the far-reaching implications of this contention. Suppose there is a local uprising in East Pakistan and the insurgents take control of the situation, does the legally constituted Government of the Province cease, in law, to exist ? The posing of this question must not be interpreted to mean that I am supporting or encouraging such a movement, for the same question may be addressed to the U. S. A., Britain and, for the matter of that, to India. No, there is no substance, from the point of view of law or of practical politics, in this kind of argument strenuously canvassed by Pakistan without taking into account its possible consequences.

Leaving aside the theoretical aspect of the question, the investigation held under U N. auspices has proved that there was no real uprising resulting in the overthrow of the Maharajah's Government at the relevant time mentioned by Pakistan, but that it was a tribal raid in which the Pakistani Government had been found to have been involved, directly or indirectly, despite their earlier emphatic denials. It is true that the raiders had been driven back by the Indian Army, but the Indian Army's intervention came after the State's accession to India with the support of the National Conference led by Sheik Abdullah.

The Indian Army, in co-operation with the State Government and the broad masses, would have been justified in the circumstances in clearing the entire territory of the State of the raiders, including the Pakistani regulars or irregulars. Instead, however, of pursuing this drive to its logical end, the Government of Mr. Nehru, apparently on Governor-General Mountbatten's advice, halted their military campaign and addressed a petition of complaint to the United Nations in terms of Article 35 of the Charter. That Article says amongst other things: "Any Member of the United Nations may bring any dispute or any situation of the nature referred to in Article 34 to the attention of the Security Council or the General Assembly." The 'situation' referred to in Article 34 was one which might lead to international friction or give rise to a dispute and which the Security Council might investigate in order to determine whether the continuance of the situation was likely to endanger the maintenance of international peace and security. The Charter further lays down that no provisions made therein for the pacific settlement of disputes shall impair the inherent right of individual or

Missing

Page

Missing Page

of certain powerful Members of the Security Council. India now is in a mess. You cannot get away from a plebiscite which, under certain conditions, is your solemn commitment. And you should not be surprised if the verdict of a plebiscite held under U. N. supervision would go against you.

Mr. Nehru has from time to time urged all manner of arguments in defence of his case. Some of those arguments are not, I am afraid, relevant to the points at issue. For instance, the Prime Minister has, more than once, stated that India is a secular country, that there are in India about fifty million Muslims in full enjoyment, along with their Hindu brethren, of the rights of Indian citizenship and that the so-called 'two-nation' theory had no application whatsoever to India and to the State of Jammu and Kashmir, which is an integral part of India. All this is ten years much too old. What, one may ask, was the basis of the partition of India? What was it that had caused such a mass exodus from West Pakistan of Hindus and Sikhs? How is it that thousands of Hindus have still been leaving their hearths and homes in East Pakistan and seeking shelter, though without much success, in West Bengal, in Assam and in other parts of India, sometimes in inhospitable surroundings and very often with no more than lip sympathy from persons in authority? It is too late in the day, I repeat, to deny that India had been divided on the basis of religion, that despite their common language, script and culture the Bengalee nation had been cruelly cut into two as if by a butcher's knife on the plea of the 'two-nation' theory and that both the Congress and the Muslim League had been, as lawyers put it, accessories to this mad and mischievous act. It is better and manlier to speak out the plain truth and own defeat than to protest and pretend and prevaricate.

An Objective Assessment

The solution of the problem relating to the State of Jammu and Kashmir is by no means an easy task. If the basis of partition is taken as the sole determining factor, then it should, in all conscience, go to Pakistan, being a predominantly Muslim region and contiguous to that Republic.

If a democratic plebiscite under U. N. supervision is accepted, then the verdict is likely to go in favour of Pakistan, whatever the prophet on this side of the border may say to the contrary. If, again, the law as incorporated in the adapted Government of India Act, 1935, is scrupulously observed, then the accession of the State to India must be recognised as a properly executed instrument. None of these courses will, however, commend themselves to acceptance by the parties concerned. All the indications, on the contrary, are that the State will remain as it is today—more than one-third under the occupation of Pakistan and the residuary under the legal sovereignty of India unless, of course, an upheaval on a world scale takes place and as a result of the impact things take a different shape not only in Kashmir but perhaps in the whole Indian sub-continent as well. 'Divide and Rule' was the philosophy of the ancients. 'Divide and Decoy' is the rule of the moderns. In building a bridge between old and new our guardians across the seas seek to combine the ancient philosophy with the modern rule in their world social technology. Partition of the State, to all intents and purposes, is a settled fact. Meanwhile Pakistan goes on peddling her precious Baghdad wares and India exports her *Pancha Shila* to earn valuable foreign currency ; and both Pakistan and India animate themselves by the eternal verities of Bandung, while some Big Powers keep their eyes skinned on this strategic region that is our earthly paradise.

Prefrential Treatment to Kashmir

In this welter of confusion the public has failed to take due note of the preferential treatment accorded to the State of Jammu and Kashmir *vis-a-vis* the other thirteen States of the Indian Union and of its possible political and social consequences. To begin with, this one single State, unlike the others, framed its own Constitution through its own Constituent Assembly. The head of the State is not a Governor appointed by the President but *Sadar-i-Riyasat* elected by the State and recognised as such by the President. It is not a *Chief Minister* but a *Premier*, on the analogy of the Australian States, who heads the Council of

Ministers. These, of course, are in a sense formal, but even a cursory glance at the Indian Constitution and the Civil and Criminal laws of the land will show to what extent the State has been deliberately kept outside their purview.

Parliament, as is well known, has power to form a new State, increase or diminish the area of any State, alter the name or boundaries of a State without its consent, but as regards the State of Jammu and Kashmir, no Bill in any of these respects can be introduced in Parliament without the consent of the State Legislature.[1] The law providing for preventive detention and the restrictions thereon cannot be made by Parliament in the case of this State ; the authority in that regard is exclusively vested in its Legislature.[2] Similarly, the constitutional provisions relating to the compulsory acquisition of private property do not apply to Jammu and Kashmir in so far as these provide for the Presidential veto through the reservation procedure in the case of legislation by States.[3] The power of Parliament to extend by law the executive authority of the Union to matters in the Concurrent List is excluded in the case of that State.[4] The Supreme Court has no power, in its discretion, to grant special leave to appeal from any judgement, decree, order, etc., passed or made by a court or tribunal in its territory.[5] The Comptroller and Auditor-General of India has no jurisdiction in respect of its accounts.[6]

Part VI of the Constitution, which specifically deals with the States in their legislative, executive and judicial spheres, provides that the expression 'State' used throughout this Part does not include the State of Jammu and Kashmir unless the context otherwise requires.[7] Nor does Part X, which makes provisions for the Scheduled and Tribal areas, apply to the State. In matters bearing on the relations, in the legislative sphere, between the Union and the States there is discriminatory treatment as between the State of Jammu and Kashmir and the other States. For instance, the *non-obstante* clauses of the relevant Articles which, in certain

1. Article 3 and the proviso thereto. *2. Article 22 (4) (7).*
3. Article 31 (3) (4) and (6). *4. Article 73 (1) and the proviso thereto.*
5. Article 136 *6. Article 149, 150 and 151 (2).* *7. Article 152*

special cases, underline the supremacy of the Centre over the States even in the matter of the latter's exclusive jurisdiction, do not extend to this State.[1] The residuary power of legislation is not exerciseable by Parliament in relation thereto [2] While on the authority of a resolution passed by a specified majority of the Council of States, Parliament may legislate in respect of a matter enumerated in the State List, no such parliamentary intervention is possible so far as the State of Jammu and Kashmir is concerned.[3]

The constitutional provisions relating to the civil services of the States or civil posts under them do not apply to the State of Jammu and Kashmir.[4] The Election Commission has nothing to do with electoral matters in that State except in so far they relate to elections to Parliament and to the offices of President and Vice-President.[5] A *Proclamation of Emergency* made on grounds *of internal disturbances or imminent danger* thereof can have no effect there (except as respects Article 354) unless it is made at the request, or with the concurrence, of its Government.[6] The Proclamation as contemplated in Article 356, that is, a Proclamation regarding the constitutional breakdown in a State, does not extend to it, and accordingly the exercise of legislative power by Parliament or under its authority in respect of the concerned State is not permissible in its case.[7] Nor does the Proclamation as to financial emergency as contemplated in Article 360 apply.

The Constitution empowers the President to hold that a situation has arisen in which the Government of a State cannot be carried on in accordance with its provisions, should it fail to comply with, or give effect to, any directions given in the exercise of the executive power of the Union. This is a normal, as distinct from emergency, power exercisable by the Centre over the States, but no such Central control over the State of Jammu and Kashmir is permissible under the law.[8]

1. *Article 246.* 2. *Article 248.* 3. *Article 249.*
4. *Article 308.* 5. *Article 324.* 6. *Article 352.*
7. *Article 357.* 8. *Article 365.*

The forms of oath or affirmation for members of a State Legislature and High Court judges and the form of oath or of secrecy for State Ministers as prescribed under the Constitution[1] do not apply to the relevant functionaries in the State of Jammu and Kashmir. It does not mean that the latter need not subscribe at all to oaths or affirmations. The point is that, unlike the other States, Jammu and Kashmir has prescribed its own forms, thereby underlining the special autonomy exercised by it.

Following the Government of India Act, 1935, India's present Constitution classifies the entire field of legislation into three categories : (I) the Union List in respect of which the Centre has exclusive power of legislation ; (II) the State List in respect of which the States have exclusive power of legislation subject to the *non-obstante* clauses of Article 246 ; and (III) the Concurrent List in respect of which Parliament and the Legislatures of States have co-ordinate powers of legislation subject to the proviso that in the case of conflict between Central legislation and State legislation, the former prevails to the extent of conflict. The residuary powers of legislation are, of course, assigned to Parliament except, as has already been pointed out, that the Legislature of Jammu and Kashmir is authorised by law to exercise those powers to the exclusion of Parliament.

Parliament's exclusive power of legislation in respect of subjects enumerated in the Union List does not extend to that State in regard to certain specified subjects. These subjects include (I) Central bureau of intelligence and investigation ; (II) preventive detention for reasons connected with defence, foreign affairs, or the security of India, and persons subjected to detention ; (III) courts of wards of the estates of the Ruler of the State ; (IV) incorporation, regulation and winding up of trading corporations ; (V) incorporation, regulation and winding up of corporations, whether trading or not, with objects not confined to one State ; (VI) sanctioning of cinematograph films for exhibition ; (VII) census ; (VIII) elections

1. *Third Schedule, Forms V, VI, VII and VIII.*

to the Legislature of the State ; (IX) audit of the accounts of the State ; (X) constitution and organisation of the High Court, and persons entitled to practise before that Court ; and (XI) inter-State quarantine.[1] In respect of these matters Parliament legislates for all the States except the State of Jammu and Kashmir which exclusively deals with them. Further, the Concurrent List does not extend to it, which means that the Legislature of the State legislates in respect of the subjects enumerated therein to the exclusion of Parliament.

The instances that are cited here regarding the preferential treatment accorded by or under the Indian Constitution to the State of Jammu and Kashmir and the extraordinary measure of autonomy conceded to that State as a special case are illustrative, and by no means, exhaustive. But, it is hoped, they give a fairly full picture of the position, status and powers of the State of Jammu and Kashmir *vis-a-vis* the Union of India and the other States. It seems, to borrow a Biblical text, that the wise men of India have rendered unto Ceasar the things which are Ceasar's and unto the gods the things that are gods'. It is for the people to judge who are the Ceasars and who are the gods—the State of Jammu and Kashmir, on one side, and the thirteen other States, on the other.

The question is, why has Jammu and Kashmir been singled out for this special treatment ? It may be that in dealing with that State in the manner Mr. Nehru and his colleagues have done they wanted to prove that their pledge that its fate must be finally determined by its own people has been fulfilled. Or it may be that the leaders of Jammu and Kashmir convinced Mr. Nehru and his colleagues that its people would not accept the Instrument of Accession executed by the Maharajah unless they were allowed to enjoy and exercise the widest measure of freedom within the general framework of the Indian Constitution. It may also be that the Muslims, who constitute the overwhelming majority of the population, were not disposed to

1. *Seventh Schedule, List I—Union List.*

leave matters under the control of a Government at Delhi which is quantitatively, if not in quality, predominantly non-Muslim. It may as well be that the special circumstances arising out of the stirring events of 1947-48 in and around Jammu and Kashmir called for special treatment. The fact is that Jammu and Kashmir is virtually a *State within State*.

Whatever the considerations that might have weighed with persons in authority in providing for preferential treatment to that State, one cannot rule out the possibility that some day or other, in the near or distant future, the other States may try to push forward, for good and substantial reasons, their legitimate claims to equality of status, functions and powers with that State which, to borrow a familiar phrase in international trade agreements, has received the "most-favoured-nation treatment" in our present political and institutional technology. Incidentally, one cannot forget the fact that the arrest of a man holding at the time the office of Premier and his continued detention without trial for so many years do not redound to the credit of the Government of India or of the present Government of Bakshi Ghulum, both of whom profess democratic ideals and claim to have set examples of democratic practice for a confused and stricken world to follow.

PART II

India from the Marxian Angle

For about two years, especially since N. S. Khrushchov's report to the 20th Party Congress of the Soviet Union in February, 1956, and A. L. Mikoyan's speech that followed, there has been a good deal of discussion as to the possibility or otherwise of achieving Socialism, as Marx understood it, by means other than an armed uprising or insurrection, particularly by parliamentary means and through 'democratic' processes. An impetus to this discussion has been given by certain phenomena which the general elections in India, 1957, have revealed. Stress is laid, in this connection, for instance, on (I) the waning influence of the Congress with the electorate; (II) the Indian Communist Party's accession of strength in Parliament and the State Legislatures; and (III) the Communist Party's coming to office by constitutional means in Kerala, one of the fourteen component States of the Indian Union.

But for the observations made by Khrushchov and Mikoyan soon after Stalin's demise in 1953, these developments of the parliamentary situation in India might not have attracted the notice here and abroad to the extent they have done. For, the fact of different political parties wedded to the basic social or institutional norms changing places, through recognised constitutional processes, in the governance of a given country is, by no means, an unusual phenomenon. It is well-known that in the U. S. A., the two major political parties change places at stated intervals by appeal to the electorate in a peaceful and constitutional manner. In Britain, apart from the historical fact that for centuries Tories and Whigs, later transformed respectively into Conservatives and Liberals, had alternately competed for power, Labour have, since World War I, pushed their way, through parliamentary processes, into political and social respectability. The precise position is that if they fail to become the Queen's Ministers they remain as the Queen's

Official Opposition which, in fact as well as in law, is the Queen's Government on the waiting list.

Both in Britain and the U. S. A., the Government and the Opposition are, broadly speaking, integral parts of the political system. These periodical changes in these two countries, which are models of western democracy—Conservatives yielding place to Labour and *vice versa* or, across the Atlantic, Republicians replacing Democrats and *vice versa*—are taken for granted. They are part of the game, and nobody is basically the better or the worse for it except, perhaps, the contestants. One thing, however, is significant, and it is that in none of these countries have the electorate favoured the Communists as a parliamentary or congressional party despite the fact that they are, without doubt, two of the most developed countries industrially and from the point of view of capitalist achievements.

Why then, in this view of the world picture, is this pother about, this *furore* about, yes, this romancing about the Indian Communist Party's parliamentary gains at the Centre and in the States and the emergence of that Party as the Government in the State of Kerala ? The answer to this question is, on the face of it, two-fold. For one thing, for the first time in history, in a big country like India have the Communist Party succeeded in persuading the electorate to vote them to office despite so many handicaps, thereby envisaging a revolutionary parliamentary possibility. For another, the Kerala episode lends support to the formulations made by Khrushchov and Mikoyan at the 20th Congress marking, as alleged, a departure from the orthodox Marxian doctrine with which the Soviet political literature itself seems to have hitherto made us familiar.

The second part of this two-fold answer I propose to take up first, for its analysis may throw light on the substance or significance of the first part. As a matter of fact, both the parts are interlinked. What, then, are the formulations of Khrushchov and Mikoyan ? Do they, in essence, constitute a 'deviation' from the Marxist or Marxist-Leninist principles ? Do they countenance parliamentarianism in theory and practice ? Can they be construed as upholding the doctrine that Socialism may be achieved by parliamentary means? These and similar other questions call for careful probing.

Before dealing with the questions I should like to invite attention to two important points. In the first place, for some time now, particularly after the 20th Congress, Soviet statesmen and writers have shown a consistent disposition to attach special importance to the principles or maxims attributed to Marx, Engels and Lenin in support of their thesis and, in the process, wherever possible, to by-pass Stalin. This trend has caused a good deal of confusion in India and abroad not because there is any doubt about the authority of the three greatest exponents of scientific Socialism but because it carries with it the implication, rightly or wrongly, that Stalin, in theory and in practice, had not been strictly faithful to the fundamental Marxian tenets. In the second place, it is not rational for a social or political thinker to rely on the myth of infallibility of Soviet statesmen and writers, however eminent they may be in their respective fields of activity. Indeed, no man is infallible and no doctrine unchallengeable.

Khrushchov Thesis

Now, Khrushchov has chosen to preface his remarks on what he calls the forms of transition to Socialism in different countries with a longish quotation from Lenin's writings on the eve of the October Socialist Revolution.[1] Lenin is quoted as having said: "All nations will arrive at Socialism—this is inevitable, but not all will do so in exactly the same way, each will contribute something of its own in one or another form of democracy, one or another variety of the dictatorship of the proletariat, one or another rate at which Socialist transformations will be effected in the various aspects of social life. There is nothing more primitive from the point of view of theory or more ridiculous from that of practice than to paint, in the name of historical materialism, *this aspect* of the future in a monotonous grey. The result *will* be Suzdal daubing". Khrushchov then proceeds to point

1. Lenin's *Works, Vol. 23, p. 58*

out that historical experience "has confirmed Lenin's brilliant precept". Alongside the Soviet form of reconstructing society on Socialist lines, he adds, we now have the form of People's Democracy. Reference to Eastern European States and the Chinese People's Republic follows with special mention of the Federative People's Republic of Yugoslavia. Khrushchov thinks it probable that "more forms of transition to Socialism will appear."[1]

That different forms of transition to Socialism may evolve within the core of Marxism is Khrushchov's first thesis in support of which he cites the great authority of Lenin. The First Secretary's second is to the effect that "the implementation of these forms need not be associated with civil war under all circumstances." While asserting that the Leninists "recognise the need for revolutionary transformation of Capitalist society into Socialist society", Khrushchov repudiates the charge that they "regard violence and civil war as the only way to remake society." Here, again, he relies on Lenin who granted the possibility, in the conditions that arose in April, 1917, that "the Russian Revolution might develop peacefully." Perhaps Khrushchov had in mind Lenin's *The Tasks of the Revolution*[2] wherein the latter stated : "By seizing power now......the Soviets could still ensure the peaceful development of the revolution, the peaceful election of the deputies by the people, the peaceful struggle of parties within the Soviets, and the peaceful transfer of power from party to party." The "conditions of April, 1917" referred to by Khrushchov were that there was no possibility of resistance being offered to the Soviets if only the Soviets themselves did not vacillate, that no class would dare raise a rebellion against the Soviets, and that the landlords and capitalists, chastened by the experience of the Kornilov affair, would peacefully surrender power on the ultimatum of the Soviets.[3]

Paradoxically, large-scale violence broke out not so much in the course of the October Revolution, which,

1. N. S. Khrushchov's *Report*, *pp. 42-44*
2. Lenin's *Selected Works*, *Vol. II p. 181*
3. *Ibid.*

relatively speaking, was a peaceful process, as after the Revolution. For that, observes Khrushchov, the Russian and international bourgeoisie were responsible inasmuch as they organised counter-revolution, intervention and civil war against the young Soviet State and forced the workers and peasants to take up arms.[1] The First Secretary is further of the opinion that the transition to Socialism was not achieved by civil war in the Peoples' Democracies in Eastern Europe where the historical traditions, according to him, were different from those in Russia.

Khrushchov's third is that the ruling classes will not surrender their power voluntarily, and here, too, his authority is Lenin. The use or non-use of violence in the transition to Socialism depends, as he puts it, "on the resistance of the exploiters, on whether the exploiting class itself resorts to violence, rather than on the proletariat."[2] Khrushchov's fourth is that the present situation offers the working class, in a number of capitalist countries, a real opportunity to rally the overwhelming majority of the people under its leadership and to secure the transfer into the hands of the people of the basic means of production. By "*rallying round itself* the toiling peasantry, the intelligentsia, all patriotic forces, and resolutely repulsing the opportunist elements who are incapable of giving up the policy of compromise with the capitalists and landlords," the working class is in a position, we are told, to defeat the reactionary forces and to capture a stable majority in Parliament, and to transform Parliament from an organ of bourgeois democracy into a genuine instrument of the people's will.[3]

The winning of a stable parliamentary majority backed by a mass revolutionary movement of the proletariat and of all the working people is capable of creating, in certain capitalist and former colonial countries, the conditions necessary to effect fundamental social changes. There is, however, a 'but' and a strong 'but' at that. In the countries, for example, where capitalism is strong and commands a large military and police apparatus the reactionary forces are

1. Khrushchov's *Report*, p. 44 2. *Ibid*, pp. 44-45 3. *Ibid*, p. 45

bound to offer serious resistance to such changes. Consequently, it is obvious that the transition to Socialism in such countries will be attended by "sharp class, revolutionary struggles".[1]

Khrushchov leaves one guessing whether, in the present-day world, there are capitalist countries where capitalism is not well-organised and who have not had at their disposal strong coercive apparatus and, further, whether the capitalist law is conducive to the growth and development of such conditions. Of course, he says that the forces of Socialism and democracy have grown immeasurably throughout the world and that, correspondingly, capitalism has become much weaker. Apart from the fact, it may be added, that the Socialist camp with its population of over 900 million is growing and gaining in strength, the ideas of Socialism are indeed coming to dominate the minds of all toiling humanity.

The question nevertheless remains, do these phenomena, by themselves, constitute an effective force to send capitalism peacefully into liquidation and undermine the loyalty of its armed servitors in big and powerful bourgeois States? To this Khrushchov himself attempts an answer, and it is his fifth and last thesis presented to the 20th Congress in connection with different forms of transition to Socialism. "Whatever the form of transition to Socialism," concludes Khrushchov, "the decisive and indispensible factor is the political leadership of the working class headed by its vanguard. Without this there can be no transition to Socialism."[2] It means that the working class under the leadership of the Communist Party must take charge, as a condition precedent to the transformation of a bourgeois Parliament into an instrument of the people's will. No such thing is within the range of practical politics, suggests the First Secretary, unless the Communist Party upholds the 'revolutionary Marxism' in battle against the reformists and opportunists as had been done by Lenin and the Bolshevik Party in Russia.[3]

1. Khrushchov's *Report*, p. 46   2. *Ibid*, p. 46   3. *Ibid*, p. 46

Elaboration by Mikoyan

Mikoyan generally follows the Khrushchov line but goes, in somewhat greater detail, into the matter in order to remove any misunderstanding that the proceedings of the 20th Congress might create in certain circles. He quotes from Marx who, in his speech to a meeting in Amsterdam in 1872, admitted the possibility of the workers of countries like America, Britain and Holland capturing power by peaceful means, special regard being had to their institutions, customs and traditions. Marx pointed out at the same time that "in the majority of the Continental countries, force must serve as the lever of our revolution ; force is what we shall have to resort to at a certain moment in order completely to establish the rule of labour".[1] He denied in that speech having ever affirmed "that absolutely the same means leads to this goal." Marx, it is contended in certain circles, thus felt constrained upon second thoughts to modify or revise his formulations in the *Communist Manifesto* in the light of far-reaching social developments. His early romanticism, it is suggested, was tempered by sobriety of judgement in subsequent years.

Mikoyan then refers to Lenin, who in 1917 observed that in the new conditions of monopoly capitalism and in view of the growth of the police-bureaucratic machine in Britain and the U. S. A. the reservation made by Marx in 1872 had lost its validity. What Lenin conceded, on the authority of Marx, was that "the method of gaining power cannot thus be the same," to quote Mikoyan, "for different countries in different periods, in different international situations". Continuing Mikoyan adds : "Everything depends on the concrete correlation of the class forces, on the degree of organisation of the working class and its opponent, on the ability of the working class to attract allies to its side, above all, the peasantry ; the institutions, customs and traditions in the various countries also have to be taken into account".

Again, Mikoyan cites Lenin as having criticised Kautsky and others of their ideological persuasion for interpreting

1. Marx and Engels : *Works, Vol 14, Part II, p. 669*

Marx's formula of 1872 in their own way, in a "reformist way", elevating it to an omnibus principle for all countries and for all periods of development and diverting "the proletariat from a revolutionary way."[1] Whatever Marx and Lenin might have said, they never abandoned the "revolutionary way" in favour of the "opportunist, reformist way." According to Mikoyan, Lenin visualised that the transition to Socialism could take place peacefully in a small bourgeois country given the existence of neighbouring Socialist countries. Further, a peaceful revolution was possible only if the working class was strong, well-organised and class conscious. In other cases, observes Mikoyan, where the bourgeoisie have at their beck and call a strong military and police machine they will undoubtedly force an armed struggle on the proletariat in order to hold what they have. In such a case, which impliedly shall be the rule and not the exception, the proletariat must be prepared to defend their interests.[2] It is not in the interests of the working class to seek to take power by violence; violence is forced on them by the bourgeoisie and their police-military machine. Lenin said nevertheless that "the working class would prefer......to take power into its hands peacefully".[3] Thus violence as such is no article of faith in the Marxian doctrine. Nor is non-violence its fashionable dogma.

Lest this presentation of the problem should give an opportunity to "would-be theoreticians, doctriniares" to argue that Marxism does not differ from 'revisionism', Mikoyan ruthlessly hauls the "reformists and revisionists" over the coals. He says: "The reformists and revisionists have always,now as ever, worked only to restrict the struggle of the working class to minor reforms, to petty concessions by capital to labour, to bring about merely a slight improvement in the living conditions of the working class under capitalism, while preserving intact the domination of the capitalist system. They were and are, in a sense, apologists of capitalism; they are not revolutionaries but evolutionaries who reject revolution and the seizure of power by the

1. Mikoyan's *Speech to the 20th Congress*, p. 24
2. *Ibid*.p. 26 3. Lenin's *Works*, Vol. *IV* p. 254

working people, who believe that small and miserly gains over the course of many years can bring them some day to Socialism. Perhaps some of them do not really believe this, but even so they are deceiving the people as if they did."[1]

Again, "There are cases of Socialist Parties having won a majority in Parliament; Socialist Governments have even existed, or exist today in a number of countries. But in these cases, too, the matter has been limited to separate petty concessions in favour of the workers, and no Socialism is being built. What is needed is that the working class should take over the government of society, that the working class should be prepared not only organisationally, but politically and theoretically as well, to fight for Socialism, that it should not be content with crumbs from the capitalist table, but having obtained a majority, should take the power into its hands and abolish private ownership of the basic means of production".[2] Mikoyan elaborates his point and observes that every transition from capitalism to Socialism, every fundamental change in social relations, is a revolution, in some cases, more acute than others, but revolution all the same. "The capture of power by the people", he continues, "the transition of ownership of the means of production from a private to a social form, is the greatest revolution in history". He concludes that "the question of the possibility of peaceful revolution in separate countries should not be confused with reformism". The working class is called upon to wage a ceaseless struggle "against reformism and the illusions which reformism engenders in its ranks".[3]

The Basic Formulations of the 20th Congress

Certain conclusions may be deduced from Khrushchov's Report presented to the 20th Congress on behalf of the Central Committee of the Communist Party and Mikoyan's speech which followed. These, briefly, are: (i) that Marxism is not a dogma but a mode of action, permitting, as it does, different forms of Socialist development; (ii) that

1. Mikoyan's *Speech to the 20th Congress*, p. 28
2. *Ibid*, pp. 28-29
3. *Ibid*, p. 29

parliamentary institutions may coneivably be one such form of transition; (iii) that the decisive factor in the transition, whatever the form, must be the capture of power by the working class under the leadership of the Communist Party; (iv) that where the country is ruled by a strong and big bourgeois State having at its disposal a strong coercive machine the transition to Socialism by peaceful means is not a practical proposition; and (v) that revolution, peaceful or other, must not be confused with reformism, from which it follows that the capture of power by the working class must be coupled with the abolition of private ownership of the basic means of production.

These documents together with Khrushchov's denunca-tion of 'the personality cult' with particular reference to Stalin's alleged activities in the closing years of his great career, the manner of their presentation, the reported diplomatic activities of the Kremlin, the Beria episode, the swift and drastic changes in the Soviet apparatus, the restoration of Marshal Tito to Socialist respectability, the Kremlin's new reactions to the overall political scenes in the South East Asia region, including its revised interpretation of the role of Gandhism in world history and of the implications of India's home and foreign policy—all these and other events, it must nevertheless be admitted, left large sections of peoples in this country and abroad in confusion as to the fundamentals of Marxism, the real character of the Soviet system and the precise meaning of the thesis approved by the 20th Congress. Especially the Soviet leaders' reference to the forms of transition to Socialism in the People's Democracy in the States of Eastern Europe gave rise to a good deal of speculation.

It is true that side by side with the Soviet form of revolution we have now the form of People's Democracy. It is also true that after taking over power, the Chinese People's Republic, under the leadership of the Communist Party, has been engaged in implementing a policy of peace-ful reorganisation of private industry and trade and their gradual transformation into a component of Socialist economy. But if it is suggested that in Eastern Europe they have evolved the form of People's Democracy as a transition to Socialism by parliamentary, constitutional or peaceful means, then we can only say that history does not support it. Without doing injustice to the Communist and other progressive and patriotic forces in these countries one is entitled to point out that but for the Red Army and its success in crushing the Fascist military machine, the social and political pattern of Eastern Europe would have been different from what it is at present.

Not only that. The Warsaw Pact is a reminder that the Communists can ill afford to forget the famous Marxist slogan, "Workers of the World Unite". And the recent tragic events in Hungary (1956-57) have demonstrated that Stalin had perhaps a little more Marxian foresight than has been credited to him since 1955-56. The fact is that the People's Democracy in Eastern Europe cannot grow and develop towards Socialism except in alliance with, and with the support of, the Soviet Union, our mechanical reliance on the famous *Pancha Shila* notwithstanding. It has not come into existence by parliamentary means and it cannot gain in strength and stature by what are familiar to us as parliamentary processes. As the result of a fairly exhaustive review of the happenings in Eastern Europe, especially with reference to Hungary, the Chinese Communists have come to the finding that in that country "a dictatorship of the proletariat had not been established" in the past. They say that those 'Socialists' who depart from the dictatorship of the proletariat and prate about 'Democracy' actually stand with the bourgeoisie in opposition to the proletariat.[1]

So far as the Chinese People's Republic is concerned, the Communist Party and revolutionary armies had fought bitter struggles for years, not in the peaceful, non-violent way; and after having captured power by an armed, sanguinary battle they have "insured the possibility of going over to Socialist transformation by peaceful means". Evidently, Erskine May's *Parliamentary Practice* has not brought

1. Supplement to *China To-day*, January 15, 1957

Chairman Mao to power in China. While May's disciples, as is their wont, proceed from the ballot to the bullet Mao's comrades, in fulfilment of the historic necessity, have gone from the bullet to the ballot.

Anna Louise Strong on Soviet Developments

Anna Louise Strong, a competent writer on Soviet and Chinese affairs, refers, it is intersting to note, with apparent approval, to certain theses of the 20th Congress of the Soviet Union's Communist Party in 1956.[1] One of these theses is to the effect that in the change from capitalism, Socialism would not necessarily take the Russian path, that each nation would chalk out its own path, maybe some nation would achieve Socialism through parliamentary forms. It was not denied, however, that in Russia the working class had seized power by armed uprising, but Anna Louise Strong seems to be in agreement with the alleged Soviet Party thesis that this method of reaching Socialism was outgrown. It was outgrown and new ways were possible because of the strength of Socialism on a world scale. It was, according to her, not a matter of speculation ; it was only a record of what had already happened in certain parts of the world.

The author says that none of the new Socialist States followed the Russian road, and she goes on to add that in East Europe Socialism "had come through coalition governments". In China, she continues, "the Communists had a coalition with Chiang Kai-Shek, and when he broke it by launching civil war against them, they had won by coalition with the anti-Chiang forces, including even the *national capitalists*". The author is perhaps correct in her apprisal of the situation but correct only partially. She is correct in so far as she suggests that, unlike the Soviet Union, the People's Republic of China or the People's Democracy in East Europe recognises in a way the existence of political parties and that room is found for representatives of different parties or individuals in the concerned governments which she calls coalitions.

1. Anna Louise Strong : *The Stalin Era*, p. 194

I am afraid, however, that in interpreting these events or in summarising the propositions propounded by Khrushchov at the 20th Congress the author ignores certain fundamentals of Marxism which have been exhaustively dealt with in the historic Chinese pamphlet entitled *More on the Historical Experience of the Dictatorship of the Proletariat*. It is of the essence of Marxism that the cause of Socialism cannot be fostered, sustained and promoted without the dictatorship of the proletariat, which, as Liu Shao-Chi points out, is realised through the leadership of the party of the proletariat—the Communist Party.[1] In China, it is not a coalition, in the parliamentary sense of the term, that is functioning; it is "the party of the working class—the Communist Party......that leads the State powers of the whole country."[2]

The first requisite for Socialist revolution is, therefore, the capture of power by the toiling people. After that will have been achieved, the vacillating forces, whether they be the national bourgeoisie or petty traders or middle class professionals, tend to rally under the flag of the victorious party. That is the experience of history. When these forces genuinely pledge their support to the working class leadership in the State and are found capable of useful social labour the task of the revolution is not 'liquidation', but moral and spiritual healing. What has been attempted in China is in accord with this basic principle.

Almost the same pattern has been the usual feature *mutatis mutandis* of the development of the East European States. In these countries, the transition to Socialism was not reached by or through parliamentary processes or peaceful negotiations. The Soviet Army, with the support, in the rear, of the workmen and peasants, "broke the armed forces of Hitler, and with them, the satellite forces"[3] of the reactionary indigenous ruling classes and thus paved the way to the establishment of People's Democracies as a transition to Socialism. These democracies, as Andrew

1. Liu Shao-Chi: *Report to the 8th National Congress of the Chinese Communist Party made on Sept. 15, 1956, p. 85* 2. *Ibid*, p. 8
3. Andrew Rothstein: *Peaceful Co-existence*, p. 108

Rothstein observes, "found the Soviet forces, and later Soviet diplomacy protecting them while they took steps to guarantee both social emancipation and national independence."[1] These are not 'Coalition Governments' but *People's Democracies* or, as Mao or Liu Shao-Chi would like to put it, 'Democratic Dictatorships' functioning under the leadership of toiling humanity.

Coalition Governments in the Western sense are the Governments of ideologically like-minded parties and act within the basic limitations of capitalist society. People's Democracies, on the other hand, having broken the main capitalist structure, proceed to build Socialism. In building Socialism, they may, of course, follow different paths in accordance with the needs and requirements of each given situation. These may be peaceful paths, non-violent paths, paths that leave no room for strife and conflict. But history does not show that the transition was, in any instance cited by Anna Louise Strong, reached without recourse to force. It does not mean that where force is avoidable the Marxian Socialists would nevertheless employ it in callous and cynical disregard of an objective situation. What they believe and what history has proved, time and again, is that the custodians of vested interests and leaders of obsolescent social forces do offer, as a rule, violent resistance to any radical change in the relations of production, which cannot be liquidated except by recourse to a superior social force.[2]

Marxism as interpreted by Marx, Engels and Lenin

It would, I should think, not be out of place to go a little more into the Marxian literature than has apparently been attempted by Khrushchov and Mikoyan in further elucidation of the historic role of scientific Socialism in the reconstruction of society and of the Socialist assessment

1. Andrew Rothstein: *Peaceful Co-existence, p. 105*

2. "Lenin...at one time thought that a peaceful development of the revolution in Russia was possible...That was the period from April to July 1917. But after the July defeat Lenin recognised that a peaceful transition to the proletarian revolution had to be considered out of the question."—J. Stalin's *Works, Vol. 9, p. 257*

of parliamentary institutions. In the course of a letter to Weydemeyer dated March 5, 1852, Marx wrote :

"No credit is due to me for discovering the existence of classes in modern society, nor yet the struggle between them. Long before me, bourgeois historians had described the historic development of the class struggle, and bourgeois economists the economic anatomy of the classes. What I did that was new was to prove (i) that the existence of classes is only bound up with particular historic phases in the development of production ; (ii) that the class struggle necessarily leads to the *dictatorship* of the proletariat ; (iii) that the dictatorship itself only constitutes the transition to the abolition of *all classes* and to a classless society."[1]

Explaining the above significant observation Lenin wrote that he alone was a Marxist who extended the acceptance of the class struggle to the acceptance of the dictatorship of the proletariat. That was where the profound difference lay between a Marxist and an ordinary petty and even big bourgeois. It was, according to Lenin, the measure of real understanding and acceptance of Marxism.[2] Anything short of acceptance of the proletarian dictatorship is base coin in the approved Marxian currency. Lenin concedes, however, that for a bourgeois State the most perfect and advanced model is the parliamentary democratic republic. But the Soviets represent a new type, and since the end of the nineteenth century revolutionary epochs have been producing that type, a higher type of democracy. The parliamentary system hampers and stifles the political life of the masses. It prevents, by various devices, their direct participation in the life of the State from top to bottom. Entirely different is the case with the Soviets.[3] A distinction must always be made between a 'revolutionary' democracy and a 'reformist' democracy under a capitalist Ministry. A revolutionary democracy is not revolutionary in word but in action ; it proceeds to the revolution and not to compromise.[4] And yet, that is, there are bourgeois States

1. *The Correspondence of Marx and Engels.*
2. Lenin's *Works, Vol. II, p. 163.*
3. *Ibid, pp. 82-84*
4. *Ibid, pp. 59-62*

and bourgeois States and their forms vary. But in essence they are all the same: *the dictatorship of the bourgeoisie.* Similarly, the transition from capitalism to communism may and will reveal a variety of forms in accordance with the customs, traditions and institutional patterns of different countries, but in essence they will all be the same: *the dictatorship of the proletariat.*[1]

There must be no mistake about the role of the revisionists and defenders of parliamentarianism. They try, as ever, to attack the very foundation of Marxism, namely, the doctrine of the class conflict and that of the proletarian dictatorship. They argue that now that you have universal franchise, the machinery of elections, certain freedoms guaranteed in the Constitutions and the rest there is no sense in shouting slogans about the conflict of classes. Parliamentary democracy, it is insisted, has eliminated the classes. For, as "the will of the majority" has it under democracy one must not regard the State as an organ of class rule. Nor should, in such a context, alliances with the progressive social-reformist bourgeoisie be rejected. Lenin calls it revisionism which, according to him, represents a fairly harmonious system of views, namely, the old and well-known liberal bourgeois views. The liberals also have always said that parliamentarianism has destroyed classes and class divisions, since the right to vote and the right to participate in the affairs of the State are shared by all citizens without distinction. Lenin repels these views, and in doing so, he says that the whole history of Europe in the second half of the nineteenth century and and the whole history of the Russian Revolution at the beginning of the twentieth century clearly show how absurd these views are.[2]

The so-called freedom of 'democratic' capitalism aggravates and accentuates rather than mitigates economic distinctions, the conflict of classes. "Parliamentarianism does not remove, but rather lays bare the innate character even of the most democratic bourgeois republics as organs of

1. Lenin's *Works, Vol. II, p. 164*
2. Lenin: *On Marxism and Revisionism*, published in 1908.

class oppression."[1] The real essence of bourgeois parliamentarianism, not only in parliamentary-constitutional monarchies but also in the most democratic republics, is, in Lenin's opinion, to decide once every few years which member of the ruling class is to repress and oppress the people in parliament.[2]

Lenin then quotes from Marx on *The Civil War in France* and says that the way out of parliamentarianism is, of course, not to abolish representative institutions and the electoral principle but to convert the representative institutions from 'talking shops' into working bodies.[3] Yes, "a working, not a parliamentary body, executive and legislature at the same time...", as Marx puts it. From America to Switzerland, from France to England, Norway and so forth, in fact all countries where there is parliamentary democracy as the instrument of the State—the actual work of the State, says Lenin, is done behind the scenes and is carried on by the Departments, Chancelleries and General Staffs. And Parliament ? Well, "Parliament itself is given up to talk for the special purpose of fooling the people". He admits, however, that one cannot imagine democracy, not even proletarian democracy, without representative institutions ; but the Communists must think of democracy without parliamentarianism, if their criticism of bourgeois society is not empty chatter and their desire to overthrow the rule of the bourgeoisie is earnest, sincere and genuine.[4] The rule of the bourgeoisie, observes Lenin, is irreconcilable with true revolution and true democracy.

In the twentieth century and in a capitalist country a revolutionary democrat must advance towards Socialism without fear.[5] Where the contradictions are irreconcilable, the conflict is inevitable, and the revolutionary vanguard of the working class proceeds to capture power and establish the dictatorship of the proletariat, that is, the democratic dictatorship—a democracy for toiling humanity but a dictatorship against the exploiters, landlords and capitalists. That democratic dictatorship, that is, the

1. *Ibid.* 2. Lenin's *Works, Vol. II, p. 171*
3. *Ibid, p. 179* 4. *Ibid, p. 178* 5. *Ibid, p. 111*

dictatorship of the proletariat, is only the transition from Capitalism to Socialism.

The observations made by Lenin in the course of his speech to the Sverdlov University in July, 1919, are significant. Lenin refers to Engels' book, *The Origin of the Family, Private Property and the State*, and cites the latter's authority in support of the thesis that every State where there is private property in land and in the means of production, where capital exists, however democratic it may be, is a Capitalist State. It is a machine employed by the capitalists to keep the working class and poor peasants in subjection. Adult franchise, Constituent Assembly, Parliament—all these are merely a form, a sort of promissory note which does not alter matters in any essential way. The forms of domination, of exploitation and of coercion may vary from place to place and from time to time, and the power of capital may manifest itself in one way where one form operates, and in another way where another form operates. But essentially and basically—and that is the most important point—the power to coerce, command and sanction is in the hands of capital,' whether there are voting rights or not, or whether the bourgeois State is a democratic republic or a constitutional monarchy. Given the existence of capital, it is the dominating factor in society, and no democratic republic, no form of franchise, no system of constitutional guarantees can alter the essence of the matter.[1]

Lenin on Bourgeois Democracy

Lenin himself poses the question as to why there is, all the world over, so much emotional attachment to bourgeois democracy and its different forms such, for instance, as are manifested in the American Republic, the Parliamentary Constitutional Monarchy in Britain and the Confederacy of the Swiss Cantons notwithstanding the cynical way in which the so-called democratic processes are used for coercing the working people and peasantry. He gives answer to his own question. There is no denying, as he shows, that

1. Lenin: *Marx-Engels Marxism*, pp. 488-89

capitalism has made outstanding contributions to human advance during the last two or three hundred years. The bourgeois republic, parliament, adult suffrage, and the rest represent great progress in the development of society. Without these, the development of the working class would have been impossible. There was nothing even approximately resembling this development among the peasant serfs, not to speak of the slaves. These facts explain why the parliamentary forms with their emphasis on elections, independence of the judiciary, the rule of law, guarantees as to freedoms have acquired such great importance in the eyes of the broad masses of people. The emotional reaction thus generated among them seems to render a radical change in the pattern of the bourgeois dictatorship such a difficult task. Besides, scientists, artists, lawyers, priests and such other people, who are in the service of capital, must consciously and of necessity defend and uphold the rule of the bourgeoisie and provide seemingly rational justification for the bourgeois theory and practice.

But there are large sections of unattached intellectuals who also sing the bourgeois music. They have no axe to grind and yet they are found in the company of avowed and outspoken servitors of capital. How can this interesting phenomenon be explained ? The explanation, perhaps, lies in the fact that they are "under the sway of the prejudice of bourgeois liberty". Ideas are awareness of, and reactions to, environment ; and environment is largely determined by the mode of production, by what Marx calls "different forms of property" or the "social conditions of existence".[1] But once formed, ideas are governed by their own laws despite the lessons of material phenomena. As Plekhanov puts it, "the process by which the ideological superstructure arises takes place *unnoticed by man*."[2] It is regarded by him not as the temporary product of temporary relations but as something natural and essentially obligatory. What makes the unattached intellectuals representatives of the

1. Lenin : *Marx-Engels Marxism*, pp. 438-441

2. G. Plekhanov : *The Development of the Monist View of History*, p. 216

bourgeoisie is the fact that "in their *minds* they do not get beyond the limits which the latter do not get beyond *in life* ; they are consequently driven, *theoretically*, to the same problems and solutions to which material interest and social position drive the latter *practically*."[1] These intellectuals constitute the most effective force on the side of the bourgeoisie precisely because of their apparent objectivity and disinterestedness.

While admitting, without reserve, the great contributions made by the capitalist system by its own law of motion to the development of human society and fully appreciating the difficulty in breaking down the bourgeois illusions Lenin asserts emphatically that the bourgeois universal equality is a fraud, that the bourgeois State, whatever its form, is a machine for the suppression of certain people by others, for the coercion of the vast majority by an insignificant minority. The landlord, he says, cannot be the equal of the worker, the hungry man the equal of the full man. So the bourgeois machine must be cast aside. According to him, the eyes of the workers are being opened more and more and the necessity for a struggle against the capitalists is becoming clearer and clearer to the working class.[2]

The question now is, should the working class and their vanguard, the Communist Party, participate in bourgeois parliaments, regard being had to their class character and the source and sanction of their power ? In his writings on what he so appropiately described as *Left-Wing Communism, an Infantile Disorder* published in 1920, Lenin refers to the German 'Left' Communist thesis that 'parliamentary forms of struggle' have become 'historically and practically obsolete', and subjects them to critical analysis. It was true, he concedes, that as a piece of propaganda parliamentarianism had become 'historically obsolete', but it was still a long way from overcoming it *practically*. Capitalism, argues Lenin, could have been declared and, with full justice, to be 'historically obsolete' many decades ago,

---

1. G. Plekhanov : *The Development of the Monist View of History*, p. 217
2. Lenin : *Marx-Engels Marxism*, pp. 438-441

but that did not at all remove the need for a very long and very persistent struggle on the soil of capitalism. Parliamentarianism 'was historically' obsolete from the standpoint of world history. In other words, as Lenin puts it, the era of bourgeois parliamentarianism had come to an end and the era of proletarian dictatorship had begun. But one viewed world history in terms of decades, and it was a blunder to measure questions of practical politics with the scale of world history.

While as a world social phenomenon parliamentarianism was *historically obsolete* the issue as to whether it was *politically* so must be determined with reference to the actual state of class consciousness and preparedness of the whole class (not merely of its Communist vanguard), of all the toiling masses (not merely of their advanced elements). So long as it was not possible, in the objective conditions of a given country, to disperse the bourgeois parliament and every other type of bourgeois institutions, the Communists must work inside them for the purpose of awakening and enlightening the undeveloped, downtrodden ignorant rural masses. The purpose, of course, was not to hug parliamentary institutions to one's bosom but to expose their inherent political and social inadequacy and their reactionary role in this epoch and also, by struggle within and without, rid the masses and even intellectuals of their prejudices and complexes and inhibitions.

Of cource, Lenin wrote all this in 1920 with reference to the German 'left' Communist thesis,[1] but his observations are valid even today for certain countries, not excluding our own. It must, however, be borne in mind that there is nothing in these or other writings of Lenin to show that he ever regarded bourgeois parliaments, even their most democratic variants, as an acceptable form of transition from Capitalism to Socialism. With him it was a question of when and where there should be a call for the overthrow of bourgeois institutions and the capture of power by the proletarian dictatorship which alone, in his view, was the

1. Lenin's *Works, Vol. II*, pp. 586-602

historically determined transition, in our epoch, from Capitalism to Socialism. Democracy, for the vast majority of the people, and suppression by force, that is, exclusion from democracy, of the exploiters and oppressors of the people—that is the change democracy undergoes during the transition.[1]

Two Phases of Communist Society

What, then, is Socialism. Marx classifies Communist Society into a *lower phase* and a *higher phase*.[2] In our present context the lower phase may be called *Socialism* and the higher phase *Communism*, although Marx himself makes no distinction between the two expressions : *Socialism* and *Communism*. What is usually called Socialism in our time was termed by Marx the *first or lower phase* of Communist Society. In the lower phase, the means of production cease to be the private property of private individuals : they belong to the whole of society. That is the production side. As regards distribution, every worker receives from society as much as he has given it, that is, according to the quantity and quality of labour *minus* a certain reduction which goes to the public fund.

It is an 'equal right' but it is, as Marx admits, still a 'bourgeois right'. For all people there is the application of an equal standard, but all people are not alike, are not equal to one another. One is strong, another is weak ; one is highly educated, another is illiterate or half-educated ; one has more children, another less, and so on. As a result, on the basis of an equal standard of distribution for different people who, in fact, are not equal, some will get more, some less, their respective shares being determined by the quantity and quality of work.

In the lower phase, therefore, the bourgeois injustice of the means of production having been seized by private individuals is removed while the other bourgeois injustice remains, that is, injustice which consists in the distribution of the social dividend according to the *amount and quality*

1. Lenin : *The State and Revolution* published in his *Works*, *Vol. II*, p. 201
2. *The Critique of the Gotha Program.*

of labour performed, and not according to *needs*. This persists because, as Marx puts it, "Right can never be higher than the economic structure of the society and the cultural development thereby determined".[1] Thus in the first phase, the 'bourgeois right' is not abolished *in its entirety*. It goes in part and only in proportion to the economic transformation so far attained. The 'bourgeois right' partially disappears inasmuch as the means of production are converted into common property. The socialist principle : "*He who does not work, neither shall he eat,*" is also realised ; and so, again, the other socialist principle : "*An equal amount of products for an equal amount of labour.*"[2]

It must, however, be remembered that these social changes in the first phase presuppose the existence of the dictatorship of the proletariat which has already replaced the bourgeois political machine. To put it differently, according to Marx and Lenin, these Socialist principles cannot be implemented by a bourgeois State which must be made to yield place to the proletarian dictatorship as a condition precedent to the transformation of society. It amounts to saying that where the coercive power of society has not been captured by the working class the taking over of certain factories, plants or concerns or the starting of new industries by the State does not by itself mean Socialism, even in its first or lower phase. For, the essence of the change lies in the capture of political power by toiling humanity. In this phase society retains "the narrow horizon of bourgeois right," and the 'bourgeois right' in the matter of distribution presupposes, paradoxical though it may sound, the existence of a 'bourgeois State' for enforcing the standards of the right—a bourgeois State without the bourgeoisie. Society, that is, is not yet free from the traditions and traces of capitalism, although the means of production have become common property.

In the higher phase of Communist society there is an end of the enslaving subordination of individuals under division

1. *The Critique of the Gotha Program*
2. Lenin's *Works, Vol. II, pp. 204-206*

of labour and of the antithesis between physical and mental labour. Labour, from a mere means of existence, itself becomes the prime necessity of life ; all the productive forces increase with the all-round development of the individual ; and all the springs of co-operative wealth flow abundantly.[1] Only then can the narrow horizon of 'bourgeois right' be left behind and society, as Marx so aptly remarks, inscribe on its banners : "From each according to his ability to each according to his needs". These cannot be brought about immediately by the mere expropriation of capitalists and landlords, by the mere conversion of the means of production into public property. The expropriation will certainly facilitate an enormous development of productive forces. Society will be free from the grip of the capitalist technique of *production for exchange* and will go over *to the Socialist technique of production for use.* Instead of capitalist economy of scarcity society will pass on to the Socialist economy of abundance. The traditions, inhibitions and traces of capitalism will be things of the past. Then in the process the door will be thrown wide open, in the felicitious words of Lenin, for the transition of the first phase of Communist society to its higher phase, and with it, to the complete withering away of the State. How long these developments will take to mature neither Marx nor Engels nor Lenin, it should be noted, could say with any measure of certainty.

To sum up, society goes over from the control of a bourgeois State to the dictatorship of the proletariat as a transition, whatever its exact form ; from this transition to the first phase of Socialism where the means of production are common property but distribution is according to the quantity and quality of labour employed *minus* a deduction for the public fund. The political or institutional set-up is a Soviet democracy but it is a State all the same with all its coercive apparatus under the control of toiling men and women and defending itself with all its might against internal or external enemies. Then society proceeds from this phase to the next higher phase in which labour will

1. Lenin's *Works, Vol. II, p. 206*

become a prime necessity of life and it will work according to ability but will be entitled to articles of consumption according to needs and in which the State will just wither away.

A slave State, a feudal State or a bourgeois State, it should be remembered, cannot wither away. For, in these phases of social development the State is a historic necessity. It is anarchism to suppose that the State may or should just disappear, and Marxism is, not anarchism. Only a Socialist State withers away because of the dialectical development of society, because the social conditions for the existence of a coercive instrument, which is the State, will have disappeared on account of the full utilisation of human and material resources and abundance of the articles of consumption, because of the necessary psychological changes in the behaviour of man and his attitude towards life, because of his ready and unhesitating acceptance of the principle, "each for all and all for one another".

About this Marxian theory of the withering away of the State Stalin made certain significant observations in his Report to the 18th Congress of the Communist Party in 1939, which should be carefully read, pondered and inwardly digested. Even when a Socialist State was going ahead towards Communism as, in his view, the Soviet Union was going ahead, the State would remain unless the capitalist encirclement was liquidated, and unless the danger of foreign military attack had disappeared. On the other hand, with Communism the State will not remain and will atrophy if the capitalist encirclement is liquidated and the Socialist encirclement takes its place.[1] Incidentally, so far as is known, the 'collective wisdom' of the post-Stalin Kremlin has not, however, cancelled this piece of the 'personality' note of the Stalinist song about the Marx-Engels formula of a 'withered' Socialist State. Nor is there evidence, despite the Soviet Union's spectacular post-war achievements in industrialisation and technology, to encourage the hope

1. Stalin: *Problems of Leninism*, pp. 656-57, 662

that, even with the increasing strength of the Socialist camp in quantity as well as in quality, the Socialist State will, in any foreseeable future, withdraw itself into a museum shell. The capitalist encirclement, visible or invisible, of the hot or cold variety, it seems, is still a great international force to reckon with.

The Chinese Communist Party's assessment of Soviet Experience

While on this subject it is interesting to refer to an article prepared by the Editorial Department of the *People's Daily* on the basis of a discussion at an enlarged meeting of the Political Bureau of the Central Committee of the Communist Party of China. It was published as a *Supplement to China To-day* in its issue of January 15, 1957, and since reproduced in the Soviet Press. The article is entitled, *More on the Historical Experience of the Dictatorship of the Proletariat*. It concentrates its discussion on the following problems : first, an appraisal of the course taken by the Soviet Union in its revolution and construction ; second, an appraisal of Stalin's merits and faults ; third, the struggle against doctrinairism and revisionism ; and fourth, the international solidarity of the proletariat of all countries. It is not necessary to deal with all these problems for the purposes of this book. What is important is that attention should be directed to those issues which are pertinent to its main theme.

The authors of this historic document say that of the successful experience of the Soviet Union there is one part which is fundamental and of universal significance at the present stage of human history. The other part, of course, is not of universal significance. Besides, the Soviet Union had also its mistakes and failures.[1] They then proceed to point out that while, according to Marxism-Leninism, there are certain common basic laws in the development of human society, there are also features which are peculiar to each State and Nation. Fundamentally, all nations pass through the class struggle, and will eventually arrive

1. Supplement to *China To-day, January 15, 1957*, p. 2

at Communism, by roads that are the same in essence but different in their specific forms. The mistake of the doctrinaires is that they do not understand that "the universal truth of Marxism-Leninism manifests concretely and becomes operative in real life only through the medium of specific national characteristics."[1] The result is that they are not capable of leading the proletarian cause to victory. The authors, however, do not forget to warn all concerned that opposition to doctrinairism must not be interpreted to mean tolerance of revisionism.

While the mechanical copying of Soviet experience must be discouraged and opposed as being a futile attempt to reconstruct society in different conditions, it is wrong to deny the basic essence, the significance of the fundamentals of Marxism-Leninism. Those fundamentals are (1) the dictatorship of the proletariat as the transition from Capitalism to Socialism, whatever be its form; (2) democratic centralism of the Socialist State; and (3) the leading role of the Communist Party in the control and management of such State. These are set out in greater detail and in more concrete terms in the document than has hitherto been attempted. The experience of the Soviet Union in revolution and construction yields the following which the authors consider fundamental.[2]

(1) The advanced members of the proletariat organise themselves into a Communist Party which takes Marxism-Leninism as its guide to action, builds itself along the lines of democratic centralism, establishes close links with the masses, strives to become the core of the labouring masses and educates its Party members and the masses of people in Marxism-Leninism.

(2) The proletariat, under the leadership of the Communist Party, rallying all the labouring people, takes political power from the bourgeoisie by means of revolutionary struggle.

(3) After the victory of the revolution, the proletariat under the leadership of the Communist Party, rallying the broad mass of the people on the basis of a worker-peasant

1. Supplement to *China Today*, January 15, 1957 p. 7 2. *Ibid*, p. 8

alliance, establishes a dictatorship of the proletariat over the landlord and capitalist classes, crushes the resistance of the counter-revolutionaries and carries out the nationalisation of industry and the step-by-step collectivization of agriculture, thereby eliminating the system of exploitation, private ownership as a means of production, and classes.

(4) The State led by the proletariat and the Communist Party resolutely opposes the imperialist aggression, recognises the equality of all nations and defends world peace, firmly adheres to the principles of proletarian internationalism, strives to win the help of the labouring peoples of all countries, and at the same time strives to help them and all oppressed nations.

The October Revolution, as interpreted by the authors of the article, conveys these things which they term basic, leaving aside, of course, the specific form the Revolution took, rightly or wrongly, at a particular time and place. These basic things, these fundamental truths of Marxism-Leninism, in their opinion, are generally applicable. They represent the core of the Marxian revolutionary thesis.

In addition to these fundamental aspects, which are common to all, different countries may, in the course of revolution and construction, develop aspects which are peculiar to them. Precisely for this reason, it is pointed out, the Central Committee of the Chinese Communist Party stated in its report to the 8th National Congress in September, 1956 : "Despite the fact that the revolution in our country has many characteristics of its own, the Chinese Communists regard the cause for which they work as a continuation of the Great October Revolution."[1]

Democratic Dictatorshp—A Contradiction In Terms ?

And what does the above extract from Liu Shao-Chi's report quoted by the authors mean ? The People's Republic of China is admittedly a dictatorship but it is a People's Democratic Dictatorship which is, in essence, a form of the

1. *Political Report* by Liu Shao-Chi, published from New Delhi by the Embassy of the People's Republic of China in India, New Delhi, October 15, 1956, *p. 28*

dictatorship of the proletariat. This dictatorship has, it is claimed, gone through the period of bourgeois democratic revolution and is passing through the period of the Socialist revolution.

Two questions arise in this connection. First, is not 'democratic dictatorship' a contradiction in terms ? No, it is not. The People's Republic of China, as explained by Liu Shao-Chi, is "the dictatorship of the masses of people, headed by the working class, over the reactionary classes, reactionary cliques and the exploiters who oppose the Socialist revolution."[1] At the same time, it is a democracy that belongs not to a minority but to the overwhelming majority—to the workers, peasants and all the labouring people, as well as those who support Socialism and love their country."[2] Following the Marxist-Leninist thesis, this distinguished Chinese Communist theoretician writes : "All States in the world are, in essence, class dictatorships."[3] But there is a difference between State and State. A bourgeoisie State, whatever its form, he argues, is the dictatorship of the minority over the majority, whereas a people's democracy is a dictatorship of the majority over the minority.

Second, since the People's Republic of China is, in essence, a form of the dictatorship of the proletariat, how is it that other classes, other parties and democratic individuals having no party affiliations are associated directly with the exercise of State power ? Liu Shao-Chi's answer to this question is two-fold. In the first place, the proletarian dictatorship implies that the leadership over the State organs must be in the hands of the proletariat. In the second place, it implies also that the broad masses of people must share actively in the duties and responsibilities of the State. None of these requirements can be dispensed with. The proletariat must strengthen and consolidate its dictatorship as a positive constructive step towards Socialism. This cannot be effectively done except in alliance with such people as are capable of embracing Socialism and of putting in socially useful labour. Liu Shao-Chi quotes with approval Lenin as saying : "The dictatorship of the

1. *Political Report by* Liu Shao-Chi, p. 28 2. *Ibid*, p. 28 3. *Ibid*, p. 28

proletariat is a special form of class alliance between the proletariat, the vanguard of the working people, and the numerous non-proletarian strata of working people (the petty bourgeoisie, the small proprietors, the peasantry, the intelligentsia, etc.), or the majority of these ; it is...an alliance aiming at the final establishment and consolidation of Socialism." The Chinese Communist theoretician concedes that the scope of the alliance as envisaged by Lenin may vary with varying historical conditions, but basically the proletarian dictatorship is always a definite form of class alliance. In this alliance, of course, the leading role is played by the Communist Party ; and it can assume leadership only on the basis of its hard revolutionary work and positive achievements.

Mao on "Hundred Flowers Blossoming"

Of late Chairman Mao Tse-Tung's great speech reported to have been made in February and publicly released from Peking on June 18, 1957[1] has evoked world-wide interest. Particularly his now-famous slogan, "Let hundred flowers blossom ; let hundred schools of thought contend,"[2] seems to have given rise to a good deal of speculation in Communist and non-Communist camps alike all the world over. Does the speech, it is asked, constitute an attempt to reconstruct the Marxian doctrine in the light of the changing pattern of social phenomena ? Is it a call for a return to the so-called Western democratic procedures and processes for a change in social relations ? Does it amount to providing, as in Yugoslavia, a theoretical basis for the advance of Socialism along national lines ? Questions like these have been raised in political as well as in academic circles.

Some commentators have interpreted Mao's speech as having served as a prelude to the Soviet shake-up in July, 1957, culminating in the overthrow of such eminent Soviet leaders as Molotov, Kaganovich, Malenkov and Shepilov. Others have read into the Soviet purge a prompt and effective Kremlin negation of the Mao thesis. It seems,

1. Supplement to *China Today, No. 12, July 10, 1957*
2. *As a matter of fact, these are two old Chinese sayings.*

however, that the commentators have been too much in a hurry in pronouncing their opinions without giving the speech the thought it deserves, not only from the standpoint of the present complex world situation but also in view of the massive stature of a man of Mao's record as a theoretical exponent of Marxism and his achievements as the revolutionary leader of about one-fourth of the human race.

What does Mao say? "Never has our country", he claims, "been as united as it is today." But then he proceeds to add that "this does not mean that there are no longer any contradictions in our society." In his view, China is confronted with two types of contradictions—contradictions between the Communists and their enemies and contradictions among the people.[1] These two types of contradictions must be distinguished from each other. The term 'the people', as explained by Mao, has different meanings in different countries and in different historical periods in each country. At the present stage of building Socialism "all classes, strata and social groups which approve, support and work for the cause of Socialist construction belong to the category of people, while those forces and groups which resist the Socialist revolution and are hostile to, and wreck Socialist construction are enemies of the people."[2] The contradictions between the Communists and their enemies are antagonistic ones. Within the ranks of the people, the contradictions among the working people are non-antagonistic.

The former category of contradictions is impliedly irreconcilable while the latter category is capable of being resolved peacefully and by discussion and persuasion. Accordingly, the slogan of 'flowers blossoming' and 'schools of thought contending' applies to the *people*; and the *enemies* are 'poisonous weeds' that must be simply uprooted and completely destroyed. In developing this point Mao points out that since the contradictions between the Communists and their enemies and those among the people differ in nature they must be solved in different ways. The

1. Supplement to *China Today, No. 12, July 10, 1957, p. 1* 2. *Ibid, p. 2*

former is a question of drawing a line between the Communists and their enemies while the latter is one of distinguishing between right and wrong. Generally speaking, underlying the contradictions among the people, according to Mao, is the basic identity of the interests of the people. The distinguished author admits, however, that drawing a line between the people and their enemies is also a question of distinguishing between right and wrong, but it is different in nature from questions of right and wrong among the people.[1]

The People's Republic of China, as Mao puts it, is a people's democratic dictatorship, led by the working class and based on worker-peasant alliance.[2] The primary function of this dictatorship is to suppress the enemies and this function must be exercised by the *working people* and *the entire people led by it.* But where the question is a question of right and wrong, that is, the question of non-antagonistic contradictions among the people as distinguished from the enemies any attempt to solve it by administrative orders or coercive measures is bound to fail and cannot but prove harmful. Religion, Mao argues, cannot be abolished by State decrees, nor can it be forced upon an unwilling people. Men and women cannot be forced to give up idealism any more than they can be forced to believe in Marxism. The contradictions of this nature must be sought to be resolved by "democratic methods, methods of discussion, of criticism, of persuasion and education." Thus the People's Republic of China is a democracy for the people but a dictatorship against the enemies to be operated by the people under the centralised guidance of the working class. It is the dictatorship of the proletariat in action.

Six Criteria Distinguishing 'Flowers' from 'Weeds'

Mao goes on, by way of summing up, to lay down six criteria to help the people distinguish between 'fragrant

1. Supplement to *China Today, July 10, 1957, p. 8*
2. *Article 1 of the Constitution lays down : "The People's Republic of China is a people's democratic State led by the working class based on the alliance of workers and peasants."*

flowers' and 'poisonous weeds.' Broadly speaking, words and actions should be judged right if they (1) help unite people of the various nationalities in China, and do not divide them ; (2) are beneficial, not harmful to Socialist transformation and Socialist construction ; (3) help consolidate, not undermine or weaken, the people's democratic dictatorship ; (4) help consolidate, not undermine or weaken, democratic centralism ; (5) tend to strengthen, not to cast off or weaken, the leadership of the Communist Party ; and (6) are beneficial, not harmful, to international Socialist solidarity and the solidarity of the peace-loving peoples of the world. Mao thinks that of these six criteria the most important are the Socialist path and the leadership of the Party.[1]

Mao has made his stand so clear, if I may say so with respect, that there can be no room, so far as I understand it, for confusion or controversy. His contribution to the Marxian ideology is in the nature of an amplification, in the light of experience, and not, by any test or standard, an essay in revisionism. The basic principles of Marxism are accepted and recognised. But within those basic principles and subject thereto Socialism may take different forms (but not the transition to Socialism which, of neccessity, is the dictatorship of the proletariat) according to different conditions and circumstances of different countries. The question, that is, of letting hundred flowers blossom and hundred schools of thought contend arises after, and not before, the establishment of the proletarian dictatorship. With such dictatorship set up and effectively consolidated the policy of peaceful co-existence with *democratic forces* inside a country is not only possible but feasible as well. As Mao says, such a policy in China "stems from specific, historical conditions in our country." Further, "since conditions vary in different Socialist countries and with

1. Supplement to *China Today, No.12, July 10, 1957, pp. 26-27.* Compare Mao's thesis with the Historic Declaration issued in November, 1957, from Moscow by representatives of the Communist and Workers' Parties of 12 Socialist countries of Europe and Asia. Yugoslavia was, however, no signatory to the Declaration (*New Times*, No. 48, 1957).

different Communist Parties, we do not think that other countries and parties must or need to follow the Chinese way."[1] There are, thus, in Marxism certain fundamental principles which are of universal application and certain other principles whose application is determined by different conditions in different countries and, for that matter, in different epochs in the same country.

New Defence of Capitalism

Now, it is argued by certain groups of politicians and theoreticians alike in India and abroad that society is dynamic, that capitalism is not what it was even four or five decades ago, that by the impact of stirring events the world over Marxism has lost its validity both in theory and in practice. Capitalism is no longer the old capitalism ; it has, it is suggested, become more humane, progressive and democratic. Their contention is that capitalism is no longer capitalism at all ; it is, instead, a 'regulated economy', 'mixed economy', 'planned economy', 'State economy', 'democratic socialism' and, if you like, 'socialistic pattern of society'. The present-day capitalism, one is solemnly told, possesses all the virtues of Socialist society.[2]

The implications contained in this flamboyant thesis are : (1) that the cry for a dictatorship of the proletariat as a transition to Socialism has no longer any relation to reality and is consequently outmoded ; and (2) that through parliamentary, democratic processes all the social wrongs may and will be eliminated and the old conflict between 'haves' and 'have-nots' once and for all peacefully but effectively resolved. The recent tendency in certain well-known bourgeois States towards nationalisation of industries is cited as an indicator of the social revolution that is taking place in capitalist society.

After World War II, Britain and France nationalised some of the big banks and several industries while in the U. S. A. many plants, chiefly in the war industries, were

1. Supplement to *China Today, No. 12, July 10, 1957, pp. 28-24*

2. Read Y. Zhilin's two articles published under caption, *"Has Capitalism Changed ?"* in issues 34 and 35 of *New Times*, Moscow, 1956.

built at Government expense. One is asked to believe that the important sectors of national economy operate not for the benefit of a minority, not for the extraction of profit, but for the benefit of the whole country. Well, where the existing industries or plants are taken over, acquired or requisitioned obviously in the exercise of *Eminent Domain* there is provision for compensation to the former owners. In Britain the owners are reported to have received over £2,800 million by way of compensation as a result of this 'social revolution.' Nationalisation, again, gives them a stable income for industries that were technically backward or were working at a loss. Further, the nationalised industries provide the means of making the rich richer. In France, for example, big capitalist concerns are charged reduced rates on the nationalised railways and given concessions in respect of the supply of power by nationalised plants. In the U. S. A. industries built by the Government at the taxpayers' expense are often sold to monopoly capitalists at bargain prices.

Capitalist nationalisation as distinct from nationalisation by a dictatorship of the proletariat or a Socialist State amounts, in essence, to nationalisation of the expenditure and stabilisation of the incomes of the capitalist firms.[1] Nationalisation is more often than not resorted to by bourgeois States as some sort of a device to save capitalist concerns facing bankruptcy, to transfer, by means of contracts, a part of the national revenues to the capitalists, to provide soft, sinecure but high-salaried jobs for displaced or discredited capitalists and, by Government regulations, to keep down wages behind soaring prices in the name of national progress.

As a specific instance of how a nationalised business or industry is used to save capitalist concerns facing bankruptcy take the scandal exposed in Parliament by Mr. Feroz Gandhi on December 16, 1957,[2] in connection with the L. I. C.'s (The Life Insurance Corporation) transactions with the Mundhras. Life Insurance Companies had been earlier

1. Y. Zhilin's *Article in No. 34, New Times, Moscow, 1957, p. 4*
2. *The Statesman, December 18, 1957*

nationalised and a Corporation set up for the purpose of running and managing insurance business in India. The L. I. C.'s funds are no longer private property ; they are the funds of the State. Now, the L. I. C. purchased the shares of the Mundhra concerns on June 25, 1957. As Mr. Gandhi pointed out, "prices were artificially created by crude market manipulations on June 24, when all of a sudden all these shares reached their peak." Immediately after the date of purchase the downward trend of the prices began, and "on December 13, the Corporation's investment had depreciated by about Rs. 3,700,000 against a total investment of Rs. 12,444,000. Mr. Gandhi was of the opinion that actually the total loss would be greater because the total investment was about Rs. 15,600,000.

Mr. Krishnamachari, Finance Minister, was forced to admit in the course of the debate that "the facts, as made out by Mr. Gandhi, were no doubt deadly." All that he could say in defence—and a poor defence at that—was, however that "the scheme......of somebody conspiring over a period of time and then suddenly dumping the shares on a Corporation, which fell like a ripe plum into the bargain, was not correct." Perhaps Mr. Dange, the Communist leader, was right when he observed that Mr. Gandhi might be surprised but that many others were not. What else he asked, could one expect from a Government "which in its main policies is advised by the private sector and some of the biggest speculators in the country ?" Yes, there was nothing in these transaction to be surprised at. The surprise, again is not, as Mr. Dange thought, that Mr. Gandhi could find them out, for being a devout Congressman Mr. Gandhi is expected to know what the Grand Council of Congress Cardinals understand by the sacred formularies of the socialistic pattern of society. The surprise really is that there should be Marxists who would reach a Socialist millennium by friendly parleys in the hospitable bourgeois-democratic parlour and who would hasten the end of bourgeois rule by bourgeois planning.

That nationalisation does not necessarily mean Socialism is proved by the fact that even the British Government in

India had felt constrained from time to time to nationalise certain industries. The earliest step taken in this direction was in respect of Posts and Telegraphs to which, comparatively recently, has been added Telephones. Then came the acquisition of railways with provisions for payment of heavy and excessive annuities to the British owners. They also set up defence industries under their ownership, control and management. The real test then was, as it is at present, who ran and controlled the State machine—the bourgeoisie, foreign or indigenous, or the working class ?

Connected with nationalisation are questions arising out of the starting of heavy industries by the State or by private capitalist firms with the support and aid of the State, and economic planning. It is argued that these are measures calculated to prepare the ground for the achievement of Socialism or at least the socialistic pattern of society as a means of building up an egalitarian society. Here, again, there seems to be a good deal of confusion. No body can deny that in the U. S. A., Britain and France they have built up heavy industries. They have in recent years gone in for planning, more or less, on a huge nation-wide scale. Are they moving towards Socialism ? In our country too, the British encouraged, though not wholeheartedly, the setting up of some heavy industries, for instance, the Tata Steel Works at Jamshedpur and gave them fiscal concessions. They did it not because, being converted to Marxian principles they chose their Indian Empire as the venue for a bold, imaginative and revolutionary experiment with Socialism but because they had to yield, in spite of themselves, to the law of capitalism and adjust themselves to the exigencies of a developing world situation. In this case, as in that of nationalisation, the real test is to whom the power to command, coerce and sanction belonged and by whom and in whose interests it was exercised.

It is claimed by certain bourgeois politicians and theoreticians that with drastic changes in the structure of capitalism and in its management and control the rich are becoming poorer and the poor richer—a sort of 'income revolution', a phenomenon discovered by Dr. Arthur F. Burns, economic adviser to the U. S. A. President. His theory of this new 'revolution' pattern has found support from Simon Kuznets, an American economist. This line of reasoning has been taken up also by the capitalists in this country and some theoreticians ; and they rely, in support of their contention, on laws and regulations regarding income tax, the operation of managing agencies, estate and succession duties and the like.

But what are the facts ? A resounding success is claimed for the First Five-Year Plan in our country, and a great future is held out for the Second. One single instance will show how extremely debatable is this claim from the point of view of our toiling men and women. The income from our industries is repoted to have risen from Rs. 550 crores in 1950 to Rs. 770 crores in 1954 whereas the share of the wage bill fell from 42% in 1950 to 33% in 1954 As regards the world's biggest capitalist countries, let Y. Zhilin speak. He says : "In the United States, labour's share in the national income dropped from 54 per cent before the war to 42 per cent in 1951. In Britain, the decline has been from 45 per cent in 1924 to 40.5 per cent in 1948 and 39.6 per cent in 1954. The share of wages in the French national income decreased from 45 per cent before the war to 30 per cent in 1952...... they show that far from any levelling out of incomes and obliteration of class differences, there is a continuous process of impoverishment of the working class."[1] Actually, however, the percentages of labour's shares in the national incomes of these three great capitalist countries are, in terms of the per capita income, lower than those calculated by Zhilin in view of the fact that over these years the ranks of labour have swelled partly on account of the growth of population and partly for the increasing pauperisation of small capitalists and their conversion into proletarian masses. The same considerations *mutatis mutandis* apply to India.

It is contended, by way of reply, that even if labour's share in the national income has fallen in comparison with that of the capitalists, there is no doubt that in comparison with earlier standards labour is better off today. It is not denied that through continuous struggles labour has wrested

1. *New Times, No. 85, 1956, p. 8*

from the bourgeoisie certain concessions and, to an extent, improved its conditions. Besides, it is true that the bourgeoisie of the colonial powers do give a share of the spoils of their colonial exploitation, however small; to their metropolitan labour and in this way create a labour aristocracy who, while prating about democracy and freedom, actually support the bourgeoisie in their colonial exploitaion and betray the cause of revolution. Further,, it is conceded that the bourgeoisie have been forced, again by bitter class struggles, to acquiesce in social legislation ensuring for labour some security, better wages and improvement of living conditions. Against all this must, however, be set the soaring prices of all essential commodities, a swelling army of the unemployed and underemployed, whose very existence rests chiefly on the employed, a spate of anti-labour legislation of the Taft-Hartley pattern, and the harrowing spectre of war.

Marxism Incompatible with Capitalist Therapeutic Processes

Now, the Marxian 'guide to action' may or may not give us a new heaven and a new earth. But surely all the plans and all the the therapeutic processes adopted by the capitalist system under different labels are opposed to the fundamental canons of Marxism-Leninism. The very fact that so many euphemistic names are now being used by the defenders of the system to explain its inherent virtues proves that it fears to hear its own name—Capitalism. It proves that it is fatally sick and has lost the confidence and buoyancy of its youth despite the finding of the neo-Marxists that capitalism's days are not yet over and that it has yet to play its magnificent innings, so that in the fulness of time such mysterious processes will be revealed as would lead society to Socialism without toil, without tears and without blood.

'Capitalist socialism,' 'democratic capitalism', 'mixed economy', 'socialistic pattern of society' and the rest are, like music, a series of sounds which call each other. The bourgeois in our time emerges into the scene as an eclectic, who chooses from each school whatever to him may be valuable and gathers from the brushwood of the various systems wherewith to make up his bundle of therapeutic faggots, taking care at the same time to denounce and reject Marxism as the cynical dogma of a frustrated, perverse fanatic.

The Communists in office in Kerala State

All this takes us to an examination of the possible consequences of the Kerala wing of the Communist Party of India's coming to office in that tiny little State within the Indian Union after the general elections of 1957. From the very beginning the Communist Party, it must be admitted, were modest in their appraisal of their electoral prospects throughout the country. They sought alliance with all progressive and democratic parties or groups to fight the general elections against the Congress and to evolve, as a condition of the alliance or in the process of the electoral battles, a minimum united programme. In West Bengal a five-party 'Leftist' alliance was effected, comprising the Communist Party, the Praja-Socialist Party, the two wings of the Forward Bloc and the Revolutionary Socialist Party. So far as the second largest group, namely, the Praja-Socialist Party was concerned, the alliance was started on the basis of adjustment of seats, later revised and enlarged to cover the minimum programme for an alternative Government. The other anti-Congress parties, Left or Right, were not in this alliance.

In Kerala the negotiations for an alliance broke down with the result that the Praja-Socialists in that State organised a front which allegedly was at once anti-Congress and anti-Communist. In other States, there was, of course, no formal alliance except that in Maharastra and Guzrat within the composite and bilingual Bombay State the Communists appeared to have made common cause against the Congress on the issue of linguistic States. The Communist Party claimed that it was possible through the elections to oust the Congress from power in Kerala and West Bengal and worked to that end. They expected to gain in strength, as compared to the election results of 1952, in other States as well and also in the Lok Sabha, the lower House of the Union Parliament. The gains they have actually scored in other States are not constitutionally very much significant, although upon a long-term view these may hold better political prospects in future. So far as the Lok Sabha is concerned, the Congress hâs been returned with a huge majority. The Congress is thus back to power in all the States except Kerala, and with a precarious majority in Orissa.

In West Bengal the five-party 'leftist' alliance has on its roll about 85 or 86 members, including the Independents elected with Communist support, in a House of 252 members increased to 256 by the Governor's nomination of four representatives of the Anglo-Indian community. The Communist Party's share in this alliance is the largest, being 46 plus 3 out of 85 or 86 members of the alliance. It comes to this, therefore, that the Communist prognosis has proved, upon actual results, 50 per cent correct inasmuch as they have yielded in West Bengal, as in the elections of 1952, to the Congress the while giving it a shock in Kerala by their electoral success.

In Kerala the Communist Party have 60 members and with the support of 5 Independents they are in the Assembly with a workable but not sufficiently strong majority in a House of 126 members increased by one being a nominee of the Governor to represent the interests of the Anglo-Indian community. For their 60 seats the Communists polled 20,59,548 votes excluding 2,74,758, votes secured by the Communist-supported 5 successful canditates. The Congress, on the other hand, polled 22,10,251 votes for their 43 seats. In Kerala and throughout the country as a whole there is evidence of the Congress's waning influence upon the people, particularly among the working class, the urban population and the intelligentsia. It is doubtful, nevertheless, whether organisationally or ideologically they are veering round to the Communist Party in a positive sense. They are confused and puzzled and are in desperate search for a way out. Can parliamentary politics provide it? That is the question.

Three Possible Courses for Kerala Government

The first point that must be borne in mind in this connection is that the Communist Government in Kerala is not a Revolutionary Government in any sense of the term. They are not committed to sponsoring or initiating any revolutionary measures. On the contrary, they have made no secret of their intention to work loyally and faithfully within the constitutional framework. Within that framework the powers of the States are restricted, much more restricted indeed in certain important respects than those of the Governors' Provinces under the British parliamentary statute of 1935. With these effective handicaps the Kerala Communist Government cannot be expected to achieve in legislation or in administration anything spectacular. All they can do is to sponsor certain palliative measures, crossing the t's and dotting the i's of the basic feudal-*cum*-bourgeois pattern of social relations in the State.

In this broad perspective three courses are open to the Communist Government. They may, in the first place, toe the Congress line at the Centre like the Congress Governments in the other States and emerge, in the process, as disciplined, faithful and devoted worshippers in the Gandhian temple of *Ahimsa, Bhoodan* and the *Charka* dialetically evolving into the socialistic pattern of society. Should they go that way it would be a case of the penitent prodigal returning to his lazy, peaceful home. They may, secondly, launch upon a programme of competitive co-existence and make, as they say, the best of a bad bargain by seeking to rid the administration of corruption, jobbery and nepotism and offer some relief to men and women toiling in field and factory. Should they go that way and succeed they would rally the unattached masses and reformist intelligentsia in their support and make the Congress sit back and ponder. They may, in the third place, initiate drastic measures in the interest of the working class and against those of the bourgeoisie, Indian or non-Indian, which, in the sphere of the State, by the way, are not permissible within the constitutional framework, and precipitate conflict with the

Centre and force the latter to resort to the breakdown provisions of the Constitution.[1] Should they choose to go that way they would prove once and for all the unreality of their plan for an alternative Government.

From the point of view of both tactics and strategy all these three courses are interlinked and it appears that the Communist Government are in an extremely difficult and, by no means, enviable situation. They seem to have for the present chosen the second way, and it is doubtful if they would be able to produce out of their Marxian blades good, fluent and exhilarating shots on a sticky parliamentary wicket. The Central Government would not, of course, disturb them so long as they would play the game and follow its rules without giving it a plausible excuse for intervention. The ultimate sovereignty vests, by the law of the land, in New Delhi and the Communist Government in this State or that, like their Congress counterparts in other States, must rest content with what I am disposed to call agency functions. For, in the final analysis, the State Governments are no better than exalted agents of the Centre. To all intents and purposes, the State Governor is the Centre's Resident Director, the Chief Minister virtually its agent and the other Ministers, more or less, its salesmen. An exception has, however, been made in the case of the State of Jammu and Kashmir where, as has already been shown, an entirely different type of political structure has been introduced.

A Mild Show-down at Kerala

Now, in Kerala the Governor has already given the Communist Ministry a mild shock by the manner in which he has handled two or three local issues. The first issue arose out of his decision to consult the five Communist-supported Independents in the Assembly in order to satisfy himself whether or not they would support the Communist Party notwithstanding their prior press statements that they would do so and the Communist Party's definite claim that they had their full backing. By capturing 60 seats the

1. *Article 356*

Communist Party became the single largest party in the Assembly. With the support of the five Independents they were in command of an absolute majority, having thereby established their right, by constitutional rules as well as by the recognised parliamentary practice, to form the Ministry in the State. Apparently the Governor was not clear in his mind as to what line he should take in the circumstances. He summoned the leader of the Communist Party and had discussions with him. Then he met the Independents separately with a view to verifying personally their press statements and the claims of the Communist Party. The procedure adopted by the Governor in a way betrayed his lack of confidence in the Communist Party. It is not suggested that the Governor took this improper action upon instructions from the Centre, but it would not be unfair to infer that in dealing with his prospective Ministers he was much too conscious of his obligations to the Centre.

The second issue arose out of the Governor's action in nominating one Anglo-Indian representative in the Assembly without taking into consultation the leader of the Communist Party.[1] In justifying his action the Governor stated that there was no Ministry in office at the time and that, therefore, the question of consultation did not arise at all. This was, to put it mildly, poor defence of a conduct which gave ground for suspicion that he was not above party politics. If the Ministry was not in office, as he argued, what was there preventing him from postponing his nomination until after the appointment of Ministers, which was imminent ? Nothing whatsoever. Again, constitutional propriety demanded that he should have consulted the person who, on every showing, was entitled to be commissioned to advise him in constituting his Council of Ministers. Here, again, there is no evidence on record to show that Central directives influenced the Governor's decision in this regard, but then the fact cannot be ignored that, after all, he was the President's nominee and holds office during his pleasure as every State Governor is and does by or under the Constitution.[2] And according to

1. *Article 333* 2. *Articles 155-156*

constitutional practice, though not by positive rules, the President, in appointing Governors, as in the exercise of any other function, acts on the advice of his Ministers, especially the Prime Minister.

The third issue is not concerned with the relations between the Governor and his Ministers as such but has bearing, in a general way, on the relations between the Centre and the State Council of Ministers. A well-known Communist of Kerala, Vasu Pillai, had been convicted and sentenced to death on a murder charge. The Rajpramukh of Travancore-Cochin—and Kerala was then included in that State—declined to exercise his powers of intervention under Article 161 and to commute the sentence. Then a petition of mercy was addressed to the President appealing to him to exercise his powers under Article 72 and to save the life of the condemned prisoner. The President, it is reported, also refused to intervene, but there was delay in executing the sentence. Meanwhile after the general elections the Communist Ministry came to office and announced their decision, amongst other things, to commute the death sentence passed on the prisoner.

The Union Home Minister, Mr. Govind Ballav Pant, reacted immediately by stating that while the President was in seisin of the matter the State Government had no right to grant any reprieve or commute the sentence as announced. Kerala's Chief Minister, Mr. Namboodiripad, said in reply that he would await the decision of the President hoping that the latter would respect the wishes of the State Ministry. He indicated, however, his disagree ment with the view expressed by the Union Home Minister. It was further suggested that it was a legal issue on which the opinion of the Supreme Court might be sought.

Certain issues, mainly of a legal and constitutional nature, are involved in the controversy. The President has power to grant pardons, reprieves, respites or remissions of punishment or to suspend, remit or commute the sentence of any person convicted of any offence (a) in all cases where the punishment or sentence is by a Court Martial; (b) in all cases where the punishment or sentence is for an offence against any law relating to a matter to which the executive power of the Union extends ; and (c) in all cases where the sentence is a sentence of death.[1] But this power of the President in no way affects the power conferred by law on any officer of the Armed Forces of the Union to suspend remit or commute a sentence passed by a Court Martial.[2] Nor does it affect the power to suspend, remit or commute a sentence of death exercisable by the Governor under any law for the time being in force.[3] The Governor has power to grant pardons. reprieves, respites or remissions of punishment or to suspend, remit or commute the sentence of any person convicted of any offence against any law relating to a matter to which the executive power of the State extends.[4] These provisions of the Constitution, so far as the sentences of death are concerned, are, more or less, in the nature of an adaptation of the Government of India Act, 1935.[5]

In addition to the above, the power to suspend or remit sentences and the power to commute punishment are conferred upon the *appropriate Government* by sections 401 and 402 of the Criminal Procedure Code. The expression 'appropriate Government' means (a) in cases where the sentence is for an offence against any law relating to a matter to which the executive power of the Indian Union extends the Central Government[6] ; (b) in other cases the State Government.[7] Normally, therefore, the power of the State Government in this regard applies to all cases where the sentence is one for an offence against a law relating to matters included in (i) the State List and (ii) the Concurrent List of the Seventh Schedule to the Constitution. It follows that the Central Government's like power is confined to cases where the sentence is for an offence against any law relating to a matter included in the Union List and does not extend to any other case which, as a general rule, attracts. the jurisdiction of the State Government only. But the powers conferred by

1. *Article 72 (1)* 2. *Article 72 (2)* 3. *Article 72 (3)*
4. *Article 161* 5. *S. 295* 6. *Article 73* 7. *Article 196*

sections 401 and 402 of the Code upon the State Government may, in the case of any sentence of death, also be exercised by the Central Government.[1] It is thus clear that under the Constitution and in terms of the Code of Criminal Procedure the authorities competent to intervene in regard to a sentence of death for any offence within the jurisdiction of a State are (1) the State Government, (2) the State Governor, (3) the Central Government and (4) the President, whereas the like powers in the case of sentences, including those of death, for any offence within the jurisdiction of the Centre are exercisable only by (1) the Central Government and (2) the President.

In the circumstances, it does not seem legally or constitutionally permissible for the Governor or the State Government to take action while the matter is kept alive on the President's files or even after his rejection of the mercy petition. Nor is it open to the State Government to canvass the issue of jurisdiction in this behalf in a court of law or to refer it to the Supreme Court for its opinion. The power to make a reference is exclusively vested in the President by or under Article 143 of the Constitution. Consequently, if the President refuses to have recourse to that Article, the State Government are absolutely helpless.

Further, even when the matter of clemency comes within the purview of the State Government, the question arises as to the legal meaning of the expression 'State Government'. It means, in law, as respects anything done or to be done after the commencement of the Constitution, the Governor,[2] and the executive power of a State is vested in the Governor and shall be exercised by him either directly or through officers subordinate to him in accordance with the Constitution.[3] An executive order of the State is not valid in law unless it is issued in the name or under the authority of the Governor.

1. *S. 402A, Cr. P. C.*

2. *Section 3 (60), The General Clauses Act, 1897. The expression 'Central Government', in relation to anything done or to be done after the commencement of the Constitution, means the President* [*S. 3 (8), Ibid*].

3. *Article 154*

Constitutional practice under parliamentary government of the British type, of course, contemplates that in causing action to be taken the Governor shall not disregard the wishes of his Ministers.[1] One may recall in this connection the Byng-King episode of 1926 in Canada which led to the Imperial Conference formula to the effect that in their relations with their respective Ministers the Dominion Governors should be guided by the conventions or usages that applied to the Crown's relations with its Ministers in the United Kingdom. The issues involved in the Byng controversy are discussed in detail in the author's *The Problem of Minorities*. Nor would constitutional practice justify the Governor in refusing to take his Ministers into consultation. But constitutional practice is one thing and a positive legal provision is another. So far as the States of the Indian Union are concerned, there are numerous constitutional provisions which do not conform to the basic principles of constitutional practice or usage which have been evolved in Britain during the last two hundred years or more.[1]

Where the Centre, on the one hand, and the Governor and his Ministers, on the other, are in agreement there is no trouble. Where, as a hypothetical case, the Governor and his Ministers are in conflict with the Centre, the Centre may recall the Governor and put a convenient and obliging man in his place and have its way. Where, again, the Governor disagrees with his Ministers, the Constitution contemplates that he may act as the Centre's Resident Director even to the extent of overriding the decision of his Ministers and making a report to the President.

In the particular Kerala case under reference possibly the only way out of the difficulty was for the State Ministry to try to persuade the Centre to accede to their request for saving the life of the condemned prisoner. There was, as far as I can see, no point in stressing, in a mechanical way, the British constitutional conventions as a guide of action precisely for the reason that they do not apply in the States except in a restricted sense and except where there is a prior understanding between them and the Centre. Nor, I

1. *Read Articles 160, 163 (1) (2), 200-201, 352-360, 371*

am afraid, could the Kerala Ministry improve matters by seeking to engage in a court battle because the Constitution left no room for such battle. Fortunately, however, the controversy has been resolved and Vasu Pillai's life saved by the President's reopening of the case and his orders commuting the sentence of death, apperently on Central advice, to one of transportation for life. The Central Government seems to have clinched the issue by making the Kerala Communist Government undertake, it is reported, not to attempt a further interference. It must be realised that once you are in the parliamentary net it is extremely difficult to break through its meshes.

These issues have been dealt with in some detail only to show that the Governments of States in the Indian Union are, in ultimate analysis, no more than the Union's agents.[1] The Governments of States are designed by our Constitution to constitute themselves into the echoes of the virtues or vices of a developing or sinking bourgeois ideology in this our epoch of a cultural crisis accumulating at the Centre. And it is neither safe nor perhaps proper to play with echoes, for the echoes are not responsible for what they may say.

Parliamentary Processes as Transition to Socialism ?

But then it may be urged that the Communist Party's electoral success in Kerala has opened up the perspective of far more resounding victories for the Party in the next general elections both for Parliament and the Legislatures of States. It has proved, it may be claimed, that the Communists may, in given circumstances, obtain parliamentary majorities and thus capture power by and through constitutional means. In other words, Kerala is regarded by many as a momentous historic event. A proper appraisal of the event involves two issues. First, the issue is, assuming that the electorate vote them to office at the Centre and in the majority of States—for the majority in Parliament pre-supposes the obtaining of a majority in a large number of States—whether the accep-

1. For detailed treatment read the author's *From Raj to Swaraj*, pp. 366-82

tance of office means, in fact, the assumption of real power. According to the fundamental principles of Marxism-Leninism it does not. For power, in terms of Communism, involves the smashing of the bourgeois citadel and effective control of the armed forces and the bureaucracy. A parliamentary majority by itself cannot give that power. While Parliament is given to talk, parley and chatter the real work of the State is done behind the scenes by the Departments, Chancelleries, General Staffs and the rest functioning in collaboration with the Stock Exchange, its brokers and the retailers of its wares.[1]

In a bourgeois State the polling booth is not a battle-ground for the capture of power but a centre, as it were, for distribution of *visas* being an endorsement for a temporary stay in offices of responsibility without power, while the State caravan passes on slowly, it may be, but surely and with confidence all the time. A bourgeois State moves by the law of its own motion, and within its procedural limits you must follow that law or else you struggle and smash it or get caught within its wheels. For if you believe in Marxism-Leninism, the only acceptable and really effective transition to Socialism, whatever its form, is the dictatorship of the proletariat. By the Marxian standard, therefore, I see no possibility of the Communist Party coming to real power, as distinct from office, under the present parliamentary system and by normal constitutional means even if they succeed in persuading the electorate to give them, five years hence, a majority in Parliament and the Legislatures of States.

The issue, in the second place, is whether it is at all within the range of practical politics for a party of the working class with no large financial resources at their command to fight the general elections successfully and obtain the majority of seats in the Lok Sabha and the Assemblies of States. A revealing statement was made on May 7, 1957, in the Madras State Assembly by Mr. C. Subramniam, the State's Finance Minister, on his recent

1. *Read the evidence before the Chagla Commission in the inquiry into the Life Insurance Corporation's investments in the Mundhra concerns.*

election experiences. Mr. Subramaniam is a veteran and distinguished Congress leader. He said that facts connected with the general elections "had demonstrated the utter futility of fixing a ceiling of Rs. 9,000 on election expenses." Continuing he added that "almost every elected member had practically to begin his legislative career after swearing to a false affidavit because it was impossible to restrict election expenses within that limit." In reply to a question put by Achariya Binoba Bhave as to how many of the elected legislators had kept their election expenses within this limit he had to admit that "only 5% could honestly make such a claim."[1]

Imagine Rs. 9,000/- being much too inadequate for the election expenses of a candidate for a seat in the State Assembly and comprare this to the *per capita* income of less than Rs. 300/- per annum ! And it is rather exciting to remind oneself unceasingly of the national motto (truth alone leads to victory) when, as a Congress Minister confesses, one starts one's public career by swearing to a false affidavit ! If Mr. Subramaniam is correct—and there is little doubt that he is—then a political party, leftist, rightist or uprightist, cannot expect to fight the elections, not to speak of winning them, without incurring a huge expenditure and swearing falsely, after the elections, that the expenses shown in the accounts had been accurately entered and properly checked.

The ethical questions apart—although these cannot and should not be ignored or disregarded by any party that stands for reconstruction of society and cultural development of the people—the Madras Minister's statement gives some indication of the huge financial liability that a party has to face while fighting the general elections. Without going into individual cases, let Rs. 10,000 be taken as the average election expenses for a candidate. In India we have more than 3,000 elected seats for the Lok Sabha and the Assemblies of States. If a party puts up candidates for all these seats, its financial liability will be to the tune of Rs. 3 crores.

1. *The Statesman, May 9, 1957.*

One wonders how a party which claims to speak and work for the 'have-nots' can collect this sum as the first and preliminary step towards a crusading campaign in the parliamentary and assembly constituencies. By mass collections ? Yes, these may be helpful to an extent, but are they not a drop in the ocean having regard to the exact requirements set against the appalling poverty of our people and the huge size of a constituency ? The only other sources that may be tapped are the Public Exchequer and the capitalists, big or small, of the 'monopoly' or 'national' variety. So far as the 'have-nots' are concerned, they have yet no access to the Public Exchequer. What remains is the judicious distribution of monetary patronage by the capitalists, and already steps have been taken by big industrial concerns for allotment of funds to political parties.

On June 21, 1957, an Appellate Division of the Bombay High Court dismissed the appeal from a decision of Mr. Justice Tendolkar on a petition of the Tata Iron and Steel Company which had sought sanction to an alteration in its Memorandum of Association to enable it to contribute to the funds of political parties. It was urged in the petition that such contributions would serve industry in general and the Company's industry in particular.

While expressing their concern over these developments and suggesting that the least that Parliament could do was to require companies to get the sanction of the court before any large amount was paid to the funds of political parties the judges held that there was nothing illegal in the respondent-company's making contributions to political funds. If individuals could make contributions, why not corporate bodies ? —asked the judges. Even if the court in this particular case refused sanction to the proposed amendment, pointed out the judges, one could not prevent the Company from reconstructing and having a new memorandum giving itself power to make contributions to political funds, as had been done in the case of some newly formed Companies. This was the main ground upon which the appeal was rejected.

The judges went so far as to admit that they were guided by legal principles and the provisions of the existing law "and not by views as to politics and morality." It amounts to saying—and we must all be clear about this—that where the legal principles are in conflict with considerations of morality the court is bound, to the extent of conflict, by the legal principles in disregard, if need be, of the considerations of morality. By 'morality' the judges perhaps meant political morality and not 'morality' in the sense in which that expression is used in Article 19(4) of the Constitution, for otherwise the judges, I submit, would be abdicating functions which are by the fundamental law of the land entrusted to them 'Political morality', again, is not a term of art, and as a popular expression it is not simply justiciable. It is, of course, a well-known rule of construction that in interpreting law the court is guided by its wordings and not, as a normal rule, by extraneous considerations.

What, however, is of special significance is the pith and substance of the Tatas' petition. According to the petition, as the judges observe, the proposed amendment to the Memorandum of Association would "enable it to carry out its objects of earning profits and running the Company more economically and efficiently." One may be wondering how large contributions from the Company's Exchequer to political parties would or could lead to economy in the cost of production or expenses of management or to efficiency in its productive effort. The riddle is solved by the Company itself. "The Company felt", to quote from the reported summary of the judgment, "that its safety, security, future expansion and profits were all linked up with the continuance of the Congress Government at the helm of affairs, and that the Company should, therefore, see to it that that Government continued in power." Thus arose the necessity, in the view of the court, for the Company to contribute to political funds.[1]

The syllogism as brought out in this interesting case, particularly in the light of the contents of the Tatas' petition, may be put thus :

1. *The Statesman, June 22, 1957*

The Congress in power means safety, security and profits for private capital (monopoly or national):
The Congress in power stands for the socialistic pattern of society:
Therefore, the Congress formula of the socialistic pattern of society is capitalism in action.

An *obiter* of a Calcutta High Court judge also strongly disapproved of this method of capitalist penetration into political affairs which, in effect, is a sort of blackmail. One is entitled to presume that the party of the 'have-nots' cannot and will not, consistently with its professions, yield to this blackmail, for blackmail involves a price which such a party can ill afford to pay. For financial reasons, amongst many others, it is difficult to visualise a Communist victory in the parliamentary and Assembly constituencies so as to ensure their entry, on their own strength, into the Central Government and the Governments of States.

Upon a careful examination of the fundamental principles of Marxism-Leninism and the latest thesis of the Communist Party of the People's Republic of China and in view of the objective conditions of our own country it seems reasonable to hold that the Kerala experiment, instead of opening the new perspective of a Socialist revolution in India, may diminish the prospects of the Communist Party even in parliamentary contests during the next general elections five years hence. It may, one may have reasons to apprehend, split the ranks of the Communist Party and undermine the confidence of the working class and toiling humanity in their Socialist professions. For, it is extremely doubtful, with the main social and political structure in tact, whether in Kerala the Communists will be able to achieve more enduring results than their Congress counterparts in the other States. On the other hand, their activities and manoeuvres may foster parliamentary or reformist illusions among the people and strike at the roots of the basic tenets of Marxism.

Marxism as viewed by Critics

It is by no means suggested that Marxism-Leninism is infallible. As a matter of fact, some of the doctrines associated with it may have left room for controversy.[1] For instance, opinions may differ on the question as to whether society or nature is dynamic or whether it is dialectical. Dynamism does not rule out the principle of continuity of progress, whereas dialectics mainly bases itself, as the process of unfolding, on the doctrine of negation. It may be further urged that, here and there, Marxism-Leninism was self-contradictory. For, if the decay and disappearance of any social system was a 'historic necessity', that is, if it was 'inevitable', then an armed revolution for its overthrow, it has been argued in certain quarters, was a piece of sheer casuistry. Conversely, if the capitalist system had to be overthrown by armed insurrection, then its decay and disappearance was not 'inevitable', a 'historic necessity'. For, reason dictates that armed insurrection may be repelled by a superior, more mechanised force at the disposal of the State. Besides, if revolution is predetermined, that is, if it takes place of necessity, then the dialectical materialism, it is pointed out, smacks of idealism in the philosopical sense. Furthermore, history shows, contrary to Marx's prognosis, that Communism tends to take deeper roots among underdeveloped communities than in highly industrialised countries. Marx thought that the proletarian revolution would be the final outcome of industrialisation and not *vice versa*, and yet the October Revolution worked differently.

Again, it has been argued that Marx confused physical urge with the economic motive and thought that man's early effort to labour for a livelihood was identical with his biological struggle for existence, thereby laying the foundation for his thesis that the origin of society and its subsequent development were economically motivated. Man is anterior to his economic and political organisation, and mind is basically a physiological process. In the earlier stages, it is insisted, man's mental activities were determined by physical existence and thereafter by social conditions. Marx, according to these theoreticians, "ignored the entire process of the

1. M. N. Roy's ***Reason, Romanticism and Revolution*** (2 Vols.) & Karl R. Popper's ***The Open Society and its Enemies.***

becoming of man before he entered into social relations." Further, Marx, they argue, forgot the fact that in an economically determined society man's revolutionary role in history is denied, that man becomes a means of production instead of emerging, in the process of becoming, as a producer, that man is subordinated "to the inexorable operation of the impersonal forces of production."

Similar other criticisms have been directed against Marxism-Leninism. To mention this line of reasoning which appears to have commended itself to a certain school of theoreticians is, however, not to endorse it, far less to canvass it. Answers to these apparently plausible criticisms may be, and have, in fact, been given on numerous occasions by famous men, including Lenin himself. It is not the object of these pages to reiterate those answers. One or two may, however, be referred to.

Take M. N. Roy. Originally a Marxist he became towards the end of World War II the founder of a new school which he called *New Humanism*. Roy quotes Marx as saying : "By acting on nature, outside himself, and transforming it, man simultaneously changes his own nature."[1] And then in support of the master he observes : "The physical being of man is not a constant category. It implies an inseparable, eternal, relation with nature, man himself being a part of nature ; and this relation—the most vital fact of man's being—is not a relation of passive contemplation, but of action which, therefore, is the essence of his being and as such determines his consciousness. The struggle for freedom from the ruthlessness of nature, as against the struggle for existence through adaptation, separates man from the lower animals. That struggle, in its turn, is undertaken by man not singly, but collectively. From his very birth (anthropologically), man is a social being. Therefore, the laws governing man's being are to be sought in his social relations, that is, in the terms and conditions on which human beings live together".[2] What is there in this statement which counters Marxism ? Nothing. Does not Roy's thesis that man is anthropologically a social being

1. *Theses on* Feuerbach 2. M. N. Roy : ***Materialism*, *p. 199***

sound genuinely Marxist ? Yes, it does. What is Roy's 'social relations' but Marx's 'relations of production'—a phrase which not infrequently the latter uses, interchangeably with 'productive relations' or 'social relations'. It is the old wine in a new bottle.

Now take Plekhanov. He writes : "The development of the social environment is subjected to its own laws. ... The productive action of man on nature gives rise to a new form of dependence of man, a new variety of his slavery : economic necessity. ... But just as the nature surrounding man itself gave him the first opportunity to develop his productive forces and, consequently, gradually to emancipate himself from nature's yoke—so the relations of production, social relations, by the very logic of their development bring man to realisation of the causes of his enslavement by economic necessity. This provides the opportunity for a new and final triumph of consciousness over necessity, of reason over blind law ... Thus dialectical materialism not only does not strive, as its opponents attribute to it, to convince man that it is absurd to revolt against economic necessity but it is the first to point out how to overcome the latter. Thus it eliminated the *inevitably fatalist* character inherent in *metaphysical materialism.* And in exactly the same way is eliminated every foundation for that pessimism to which, as we saw, consistent *idealist* thinking leads of necessity. The individual personality is only foam on the crest of the wave, men are subjected to an iron law which can only be discovered, but which cannot be subjected to the human will, said George Büchner. No, replies Marx : Once we have *discovered* that iron law, it depends on us to overthrow its yoke, it depends on us to make *necessity* the obedient slave of *reason*.... I am a worm, says the idealist. I am a worm while I am ignorant, retorts the dialetical materialist ; but I am a god when I *know. Tantum possumus, quantum schimus* (we can do as much as we know) !"[1]

Scientifically, it is not true that man is born free and that everywhere he is in chains. What is really correct is

1. G. Plekhanov : *The Development of the Monist View of History,* pp. 273-75

that man is born to ignorance and to necessity. It is for him as a social being and a tool-making animal to dispel that ignorance and break that necessity. Therein lies his freedom, his emancipation. I need not detain the reader here over further interpretation of Marxism, nor should one in this connection take serious notice of the New Delhi Great Mougul's pompous but poor piece that Marx is a century much too old or that, to attempt a more intimate analogy, Gautama Buddha or Emperor Asoka is more than two centuries behind the clock. But the criticisms directed against Marxism nevertheless raise points upon which there may legitimately be a good deal of intelligent and instructive controversy and which may quite reasonably provoke varied reactions. It does, however, nobody good to be dogmatic. Cicero was not far wrong when he said : "All may err : but fools only persist in error."

Neither Eldorado nor Innocuous Mouse

Those who take their stand, in theory as well as in practice, on Marxism-Leninism must not distort what they swear by. Nor are they to apply it mechanically without taking into account the environment, the objective conditions and circumstances. That is why, again and again, both Marx and Lenin have denounced doctrinairism no less than the gross betrayal of the faith. Think of a concert. There is the orchestra composed of all kinds of instruments, and each has its peculiar tone. In response to the movement of time each note, sharp or flat, goes into a wave and presents itself to your ears. You hear simultaneously all the diatonic sounds and chromatic changes and yet your ears with all their fine, quiet sensitiveness distinguish the difference. That is how the disciples and students of Marx and Lenin should and must react to the Babel of voices and then pick and choose.

A deaf one cannot judge of the symphonies of a Beethhoven nor a blind one criticise the frescoes of a Michael Angelo. Marxist-Leninist Socialism is neither the Eldorado of the Spanish dreamer nor the little innocuous mouse brought forth into this care-worn world in the throes of a parliamentary reverie. It is a guide to action, a revolutionary action at that. That guide to action may take two different forms according to the Marxian doctrine regard being had to the circumstances of each given situation.[1] First, where the workers' party cannot seize power on account of the immaturity of objective conditions "its fight awakens class consciousness and thereby prepares for the revolution". That is the argument of the radical wing. Second, there may be periods in which "the forces of the two opposing classes are approximately in equilibrium" and in which "political effort and energy may be decisive in achieving significant improvements for the workers". This is the argument advanced by the moderate wing. It cannot be denied, however, that this latter point of view "sacrifices some of the fundamental positions" of the Marxian theory. But whichever form the guide to action may take, it seems a plausible answer to the doctrine of the fundamental impotence of politics as against the inexorable social reality. Philosophers, as Marx put it, have interpreted the world in various ways ; the point is to change it, and by changing nature man changes himself. Who has ever seen a sower casting his seed among weeds ? And Marx was certainly a great sower.

1. Karl R. Pepper : *The Open Society and its Enemies*, pp. 309-310

PART III

Commonwealth Partnership : A Living Reality

The Congress-led Struggle Leads to Compromise

The question as to whether or not it is desirable or necessary to sever India's connection with the British Commonwealth has agitated the Indian public mind for a fairly long time. The tempo of demand or severance of the country's relationship with the Commonwealth had, of late, been accelerated by the British Government's recent misadventure in the Suez and their sponsoring of the Security Council's decision, once again, to put India on the dock over Jammu and Kashmir, although it appears that the basic unity of the Commonwealth partnership has put a quietus to the emotional hostility to British connection. Despite Congress propaganda, however, large sections of Indian opinion have refused to acknowledge that the status the country enjoys today is basically different from that of the Dominions within the Commonwealth. The Indian National Congress, it may be recalled, officially voted for complete independence at the Lahore Session in December 1929, when Pandit Jawaharlal Nehru took over from his famous father as the President of that national organisation.

When the Congress voted for complete independence it demanded what, in theory and in practice, complete independence meant. It was not a vote for Dominion status or Commonwealth partnership. The Congress at that time and right up to the date of Netaji Subhas Bose's break with that organisation in 1938-39 was, more or less, an anti-imperialist national front representing, as it did, different shades of political opinion as well as divergent indigenous class interests from the near-feudal landlord to the rack-rented peasant, from the new Indian bourgeoisie to the toiling working class. The leadership of this front was apparently in the hands of the petty-bourgeois and intellectuals, although from behind the scenes the growing Indian bourgeoisie played no insignificant role, if of a somewhat dubious and opportunist character. Their role was 'dubious and opportunist' because while controlling the Congress's purse-strings they strove their utmost to keep the 'extremists' on the 'right track', so that they could help the Congress leadership to bargain, to their advantage, for compromise with the British whenever opportunity presented itself. On the whole, the Indian bourgeoisie adopted a 'double-standard'—toeing the British line in open, and, in secret, making contributions to the Congress Party's funds.

It seems pertinent to refer here to the observations contained in Lenin's Report presented, on behalf of the Commission on the National and Colonial Questions, to the Second Congress of the Communist International on July 26, 1920.[1] Explaining why it had been felt necessary to incorporate in the preliminary theses M. N. Roy's supplementary theses Lenin said : "We discussed whether it would be correct, in principle and in theory, to state that the Communist International and the Communist parties must support the bourgeois-democratic movement in backward countries. As a result of our discussion, we arrived at the unanimous decision to speak of the 'national-revolutionary' movement rather than the 'bourgeois-democratic' movement. ... It would be utopian to believe that proletarian parties, if indeed they can arise in these backward countries, could pursue communist tactics and a communist policy without establishing definite relations with the peasant movement and without giving it effective support. But it was objected that if men speak of the bourgeois-democratic movement, we shall be obliterating all distinction between the reformist and the revolutionary movement. Yet that distinction has been very clearly revealed of late in backward and colonial countries, for *the imperialist bourgeoisie is doing everything within its power to implant a reformist movement among the oppressed nations too. There has been a certain rapproachment between the*

1. Lenin : *The National—Liberation Movement in the East*, pp. 265-66 & J. Stalin : *Works*, Vol. 9, pp. 236-42.

bourgeoisie of the exploiting and colonial countries, so that very often—even in most cases, perhaps—where the bourgeoisie of the oppressed countries does support the national movement, it at the same time works hand in glove with the imperialist bourgeoisie, that is, joins forces with it against all revolutionary classes (italics mine). This was irrefutably demonstrated in the Commission and we decided that the only correct thing was to take this distinction into account and in nearly all cases substitute the term *national-revolutionary* for the term *bourgeois-democratic*."

This important point of distinction was raised in Roy's supplementary theses with special reference to India and China, and it was upheld in the Commission with Lenin's whole-hearted approval In Lenin's view, therefore, the imperialist bourgeoisie try, in the first place, at a particular phase of capitalist development, to foster, nurse and sustain a reformist movement in colonial countries as a counterpoise to revolutionary movements. In the second place, a sort of agreement is arrived at between the imperialist bourgeoisie and the bourgeoisie of the underdeveloped and colonial countries to suppress or crush the revolutionary masses. The history of British rule in India, particularly at the turn of this century, had convincingly proved these trends. And it is not perhaps unreasonable to hold that the British deed of transfer of power in 1947, and the continuance of our Commonwealth membership are events which have been considerably influenced by them.

It has been suggested that the Congress wrested power from the British in 1947, by peaceful and non-violent means, in accordance with the policy and programme of Gandhiji as laid down from time to time since 1920, when the non-co-operation movement had been started for the first time. It has also been suggested that the Gandhian adherence to truth and *ahimsa* was a weapon which the British could not tackle effectively, that precisely for that reason it brought about a change of heart among the ruling circles in Britain, that in consequence thereof they decided to quit leaving the charge of Indian affairs to Indian leaders, and that since the transfer of power the Indo-British relations have been placed on a footing of equality informed and inspired by mutual regard for each other's interests and the principle of give and take.

It is true that in certain stages, broadly speaking, the Congress was a liberation movement, but the claims made by its present exponents referred to above do not bear critical scrutiny. The Congress as an organisation at its higher levels had been put out of action by the British in 1942 when Governor-General Linlithgow had caused its leaders, including Gandhiji, Saidar Patel and Pandit Nehru to be arrested and placed in custody for what reasons one need not speculate upon today. It is significant, however, that two eminent Congress leaders—Mr. M. S. Aney and Mr. N. R. Sarker—were parties to the Governor-General's action which, on the face of it, was so drastic. These two together with Mr. Homi Mody, another Indian collaborator with Linlithgow, were entrusted with offices of great trust and responsibility by the Congress leadership after the transfer of power. It is clear that the Congress leaders' withdrawal from the confusing scenes of 1942 saved them from an embarrassing position, for sporadic uprisings of a violent character occurred thereafter, which they took the earliest opportunity subsequently to repudiate. These leaders were released after the defeat of Hitlerite Germany and soon after negotiations with them were initiated by Governor-General Wavell which, under the leadership of his successor, Lord Mountbatten, led to the partition of India, and the setting up of two newly created independent Dominions.

In between the time of arrest and imprisonment of Indian leaders and the date of transfer of power—approximately a period of five years—certain world-shaking events had taken place, for instance, Hitler's debacle at Stalingrad; the upheavals in South-East Asia leading to the undermining of British prestige, influence and authority as a world economic and military power; the impending defeat of Japan; the rapid progress of the liberation movements in Eastern Europe; and the increasing tempo of the Communist movement in China foreshadowing the inevitable fall of Chiang and his Kuomintung clique. The astute but panic-stricken British sensed a grave danger and so did the opportunist Indian bourgeoisie, Hindu as well as Muslim, and this sensing of danger provided the greatest common measure of agreement between the British, the Congress and the Muslim League, and a deed of partition and transfer of power was hurriedly gone through and agreed upon. The people's movement of liberation in South-East Asia was thus halted and a situation was created in which Asians were induced to fight Asians on the exciting platform of national sovereignty. Unless all these facts are borne in mind and carefully studied one cannot attempt a correct answer to the puzzling question why India and, for that matter, Pakistan, while declaring themselves independent sovereign Republics, show so much reluctance to terminate their membership of the British Commonwealth.

The Pattern of Commonwealth Development

The question of India's severance of connection with the Commonwealth may be examined from three standpoints : (i) legal ; (ii) economic ; and (iii) political, which *inter alia* includes, of course, military and strategic considerations. As to (i) and (iii), which may be taken together, it is admitted that the Commonwealth, both in form and content, is a flexible, as distinguished from rigid, concept. Roughly, the history of the Commonwealth and Empire may be divided into four periods according to the nature and character of capitalist exploitation and domination.

The first period, covering the centuries from the reign of Queen Elizabeth I right up to 1867, was marked by direct and unabashed colonial rule. Allegiance was to the British Crown ; the laws, ordinances and regulations emanated from the Crown or Parliament with variations to suit local conditions ; and the local peoples had no power whatsoever in regard to taxation, law-making and property.

Meanwhile in 1776 the Americans gave the British a shock by a successful armed rebellion against their rule and declaration of Independence on the basis of complete severance of connection with the latter. Events moved on rather swiftly and a new bourgeoisie emerged in the

Canadian provinces. There were frequent conflicts not only between the interests of the United Kingdom and those of the local European community in Canada but also between different sections of the European community itself. The year 1837 witnessed armed uprisings in both Upper and Lower Canada and then in 1839 Lord Durham made his famous Report which "was the starting point in the process that has led to the latest developments." In 1864 a conference of delegates of the province of Canada and the maritime provinces evolved a scheme of union and adopted a series of resolutions. In 1865 a meeting took place in London between the representatives of Canada, Nova Scotia and New Brunswick on one side and those of the United Kingdom on the other. An agreement was reached as regards the terms of an Act of Parliament. The Act was enacted by the British Parliament the following year, which has come to be known as the British North America Act, 1867.[1] It set up a Canadian federation and conferred upon it a substantial measure of internal sovereignty. It is significant to note that this deed of transfer of power came almost immediately after, and almost in the wake of, the American Civil War of the 'sixties of the last century.

A little more than three decades after, that is, at the turn of this century the Australian colonies were transformed by a British Act into a Commonwealth—the second act of the series in the progressive realisation of Commonwealth partnership. A conference of Australian Premiers was held in Melbourne in 1899. A compromise was agreed upon and certain constitutional principles accepted with several subsequent changes to meet the requirements of New South Wales. The draft constitution was referred to the people of each of the colonies. It was endorsed by Victoria, South Australia and Tasmania and, after some opposition, also by New South Wales and Queensland. A delegation from Australia went to London to discuss with the British Government the proposals contained in the draft. A Bill was sponsored in the British Parliament and the Common-

1. *30 Vict., C. 3, since amended in 1875, 1907, 1915 and 1930*

wealth of Australia Act, 1900 emerged.[1] By and under a Royal Proclamation of September 17, 1900, the constitution came into operation on January 1, 1901. It created a federation under the name of the Commonwealth of Australia.

The third act of transfer took place in 1909 when the Union of South Africa was admitted to internal sovereignty under the Crown's allegiance. A draft South African constitution evolved out of a series of meetings in convention held at Bloemfontein. Recourse was had to a referendum, and an overwhelming majority voted for the Union. By June, 1909, the draft was accepted by each of the four colonies. It was then submitted to the British Parliament, as in the other previous cases. Delegates from these colonies went to England to plead their case. A Bill was sponsored in Parliament, more or less, on the basis of the draft, and passed into law as the Union of South Africa Act, 1909.[2] No reference is perhaps necessary to New Zealand and Newfoundland, the latter having been absorbed several years ago in the Dominion of Canada, to explain and elucidate the flexible character of the British Commonwealth and Empire and the evolutionary processes of partnership.

These years from 1867 to 1909 cover the second period which was marked by increasing British collaboration with the white colonial bourgeoisie. It was a three-pronged process. It was designed to (i) expand and consolidate the area of capitalist exploitation, (ii) satisfy the aspirations of the white colonial bourgeoisie on the basis of joint enterprise with the British as a major partner to provide a safeguard against a possible repetition of the events culminating in the independence of the American colonies and (iii) increase and enlarge the periphery of the Empire's offensive and defensive system.

Meanwhile a violent, insurrectionary movement for national liberation was organised in Ireland and in the midst of World War I the British made a compromise on the basis of partition of the islands into Northern and Southern Ireland—a less exciting rehearsal of the Indian drama in 1947.

1. *63 and 64 Vict., C. 12, since amended in 1907, 1910 and 1929*
2. *9 Edw VII., C. 9*

Northern Ireland was retained as a British colony with provision for a local legislature and its representation in Westminster. The south was transformed into what came to be known as the Irish Free State.

By virtue of the powers conferred by the Statute of Westminster, 1931,[1] the Free State introduced sweeping changes in its original constitution. It was, of course, open to its Parliament to amend the constitution of 1922, subject to the terms of the Irish Treaty of 1921. But power was reserved to the Governor-General to refuse assent to, or reserve for Royal consideration, legislation enacted by the Irish legislature. In 1933 the Free State repealed such provisions as prohibited changes contrary to the Treaty as well as those relating to the Governor-General's reserve powers. In 1936 legislation was enacted deleting from the constitution all references to the King and the Governor-General, although by a separate Act known as the External Relations Act provision was made for the exercise by the King of certain functions relating to external relations.

In 1937 the Free State declared itself to be a "sovereign, independent, democratic State." The head of the State was called the President, although the allegiance to the Crown in regard to external affairs was not disturbed or done away with. It is significant that these changes were not interpreted by the other Commonwealth Governments as having affected the position of Eire (formerly the Irish Free State) as a member of the Commonwealth. In 1939, Ireland refused to align itself with the British in World War II, thus creating for the first time the precedent that a part of the Crown's Dominions could, in law and in fact, remain neutral when the Crown was involved in war. It was only in 1949 that Eire was declared to have ceased to be part of the Queen's dominions, subject, however, to certain reservations relating to the British Nationality Act of 1948.[2]

1. *22 Geo. V, C. 4.*

2. *12 & 13 Geo. VI., C. 41, ss. 1(1), and S. 8*

Earlier in 1931, the British Parliament had enacted the Statute of Westminster (already referred to) which accorded Dominion status to (1) Canada, (2) Australia, (3) New Zealand, (4) South Africa, (5) The Irish Free State and (6) Newfoundland.[1] This Act incorporated, in effect, the famous Balfour formula as to the equality of status of the Dominions and Britain both in regard to their internal and external affairs. It declared that they were not subordinate one to another in any aspect of these relations, although they were united by their common allegiance to the Crown and the Crown was the symbol of the free association of the Member-States. It should be noted that the Statute of Westminster created no new rights or obligations; it only gave statutory recognition to certain conventions and usages established in the course of years of collaboration between the metropolis and the outlying parts of the British Commonwealth and Empire. The third period, which extended from the end of World War I, was marked by a large accretion of power by the Dominions as minor partners in the capitalist enterprise on the basis of common allegiance to the Crown.

We are now in the midst of the fourth period which has already witnessed the emergence of India (1950) and Pakistan (1956) as Republics within the Commonwealth and the admission of an African Colony, namely, Ghana, and what Prime Minister Macmillan is pleased to call "the new independent Kingdom of Malaya"[2], to Commonwealth status (1957). The Commonwealth and Empire now comprises: (a) the Commonwealth States, e. g, Britain, Canada, Australia, New Zealand, South Africa, India, Pakistan, Ceylon, Ghana (formerly Gold Coast) and "the independent Kingdom of Malaya" and (b) the Colonies, such as West Indies, Mauritius, etc. Of the former India and Pakistan are Republics owing, unlike the rest, no formal allegiance to the British Crown, and it may be that before long Ceylon will follow suit.

---

1. *22 Geo. V., C. 4, S. 1*

2. Mr. Macmillan's *speech at New Delhi banquet on January 9, 1958*

The Juridical Nature of India's Association with the Commonwealth

Legally, of course, India, like any other Commonwealth State, is free to come out of the Commonwealth. No British law extends to India unless it is re-enacted as an Indian statute by the appropriate Indian Legislature. But the Queen has been recognised in a solemn declaration as "the symbol of the association of its independent member-nations and as such the Head of the Commonwealth." This recognition finds expression in a *communique* issued by the Commonwealth Prime Ministers' Conference from London in April, 1949, previously referred to.

What, then, does that declaration mean? It is not a purely formal affair. In fact and perhaps also in law, India's continued membership of the Commonwealth and her acceptance of the British Queen as the symbolic head of that body mean something more than they are intended to convey. In the first place, unlike the American colonies in 1776, Burma in 1948[1] and Eire in 1949,[2] India has made no provision by statute or declaration that she has ceased to be part of the Queen's dominions, thereby giving rise to doubt as to the Republic's precise legal and constitutional position *vis-a-vis* the Queen. It is, of course, true that the Queen's prerogatives have been impliedly done away with by certain provisions of the Constitution of 1950. But these, by themselves, do not eliminate the Queen, nor does the naming of India as a Republic improve the position, as would be clear from the Irish Republic's continued allegiance to the Crown, until 1949, in respect of its foreign relations and the protection of its citizens abroad as British subjects. It is nevertheless admitted that Indian citizens are protected by the Indian Republic and not by the British Crown in foreign lands. But the question remains as to whether India and, for the matter of that, any other Commonwealth State are competent to engage in war with one another or participate, directly or indirectly, in

1. *11 Geo. VI, C. 3, S. 1*
2. *No. 22 of 1948 (Eire), and 12 & 13 Geo. VI. C. 41, S. 1*

belligerent activities against a member-Commonwealth State when the latter may be at war with a foreign State.

In recent years there have been speculations even in responsible quarters about the possibility of war between India and Pakistan over Jammu and Kashmir.[1] They are evidently under the illusion that from the strategic point of view India and Pakistan are two different units. In fact and also perhaps by common understanding they are not. Apart from political and military considerations which, in my judgment, rule out a large-scale war between these two countries, I think that legally there can be no war between them unless the one or the other breaks away from the Commonwealth. Commonwealth membership does not prohibit neutrality in a war in which another Commonwealth State may be involved with a foreign State, but a war between a Commonwealth State and a Commonwealth State is, I am convinced, out of the question from the standpoint of law. Incidentally, I should like to point out that all talk of war on this side or on the other over Jammu and Kashmir is bunkum. It looks like dangling the proverbial carrot before the donkey. In pursuance of their overall strategy directed against Communism Britain and the U. S. A. would not allow the *status quo* to be seriously disturbed, and both India and Pakistan—the latter more directly perhaps—are much too tied down to the apron-strings of the international anti-Communist crusadeers. The partition of that State is a settled fact unless a Third World War unsettles it as it is bound to unsettle many other things.

And that is not all. Reference may be made, for further elucidation of the implications of Commonwealth membership, to article 367 (3) of the Constitution of India. An order known as the Constitution (Declaration as to Foreign States) Order was issued by the highest executive authority in India in 1950, declaring the Commonwealth States not to be foreign States for the purposes of the

1. Incidentally Sheikh Abdullah's continued detention without trial for four years, to which reference had been made earlier in the body of the text, was terminated by order of the Kashmir Government on January 8, 1958.

Constitution. The result is that to us Burma is a foreign State but not Canada ; that China is a foreign State but not Britain ; that the Soviet Union is a foreign State but not Australia. That means that citizens of the Commonwealth States are not aliens or foreigners in this country and as such they are, as a rule, exempted from the liabilities, obligations and restrictions to which foreigners or aliens are subject except where, as in the case of Pakistan and South Africa, provisions to the contrary are made.[1]

This constitutional provision follows the precedent created by the British Nationality Act, 1948, which lays down that a citizen of the United Kingdom and Colonies or a citizen of any Commonwealth country shall, by virtue of such citizenship, have the status of a British subject. Any person having the aforesaid status may be known either as a British subject or a Commonwealth citizen. Accordingly, the expression 'British subject' and the expression 'Commonwealth citizen' shall have the same meaning.[2] In 1949, another Act was passed by the British Parliament. It is known as the India (Consequential Provisions) Act, 1949. It provides that, on or after the date of India's becoming a Republic, all existing British law, whether being a rule of law or a provision of an Act of Parliament or of any other enactment or instrument whatsoever, shall have the operation in relation to India, and to persons or things in any way belonging to, or connected with, India as it would have had if India had not become a Republic.[3]

As regards Pakistanis, it would be wrong to conclude from the amendment referred to above that they are foreigners for the purposes of the Constitution. The scope of the amendment, further, is extremely restricted as would be clear from the Press Note issued on January 10, 1958, by the Indian High Commission accredited to Pakistan. The Note *inter alia* says : "Pakistani nationals,

1. *Read the recent amendment of the Foreigners Registration Act*
2. *S. 1 (1), (2) and (3)*
3. *12, 13 and 14 Geo. VI. C. 92. S. 1 (1)*

however, are not required to follow the elaborate procedure of registration as laid down under the Registration of Foreigners Rules, 1939. The Government of India has decided that the officer in charge of the checkpost should grant only a temporary residential permit for two weeks, for example, for 'B' category visas, or for the period of stay specified in the visa if that period is less than two weeks, to Pakistani nationals at the time of entry. The rules provide that a Pakistani national may thereafter obtain a regular residential permit from the registration office, i. e., the Deputy Commissioner, Security Control, in Calcutta, and Superintendents of Police in districts. In case where a Pakistani national visits more than one district a regular residential permit has to be obtained from the Registration Officer of the filing district of his visit."

In a special article contributed to the *Republic Supplement* of the *Statesman* published on January 26, 1958, Mr. C. Rajagopalachari remarks : "If you can swallow your pride and be in the British Commonwealth—for in spite of the change in nomenclature it is still British and its head is the British Sovereign—surely you can stomach it in the case of the English language which is your own once you have mastered it, and which has served you so well in every way and *carries no strings with it as does the Commonwealth*" (italics mine). So the Indian Republican cat has been let out of the British Commonwealth bag by this outstanding Congress leader and Gandhiji's right-hand man. I need not multiply instances in support of the dubious position in which India has been placed in relation to Britain in particular and the Commonwealth generally. It is clear that the Commonwealth membership is not a fiction ; it is a grand inexorable and pervasive reality. It is an experiment in reciprocity, a delicate political mechanism of collaborationist strategy.

The Economic Consequences of the Commonwealth

Coming now to the economic aspects of the Commonwealth membership, it is pertinent to refer to the Indian Republic's international investment or debtor/creditor position. At the end of 1953, the country's long-term foreign liabilities (obligations maturing beyond a year) amounted to Rs. 1,056 crores, while its long-term foreign assets aggregated Rs. 1,175 crores. The official sector owed Rs. 583 crores. The liabilities of that sector comprise mainly (1) the security of the Centre, the States and the Local authorities owned abroad (Rs. 254 crores) ; (2) the capitalised value of the Government's pensionary liability to retired British nationals (Rs. 181 crores) ; and (3) official loans payable abroad (Rs. 138 crores).

Most of the liabilities of the private sector (Rs. 419 crores) took the shape of foreign business investment. Of these, over 80% (Rs. 349 crores) belongs to the 'direct' investment category. This consisted of Rs 252 crores invested in the branches of foreign firms and companies (including banks and insurance companies) and Rs. 117 crores of foreign ownership (accompanied by control) of ordinary shares in Indian Joint-Stock Companies. The bulk of the 'portfolio' investment (foreign ownership without any accompanying control) was in the shape of equity capital (Rs. 58 crores). The two individual lines of business activity in which there was substantial foreign capital were tea plantations and trading in petroleum products, with a net foreign investment of Rs. 71 crores and Rs. 67 crores respectively.

Business investments from Britain (Rs. 347 crores) constituted over 80% of the total foreign investments in the country. The U. S. A. was the next important country in this respect, with a total investment of Rs. 31 crores. A substantial portion of the investment from both Britain and the U. S. A. was of the 'direct' category (accompanied by control). Addressing a Press Conference at New Delhi on January 11, 1958, Mr. Macmillan, Britain's Prime Minister, quoted from the Reserve Bank of India's recent publication on foreign investments and claimed that his country was far ahead of other countries in respect of investments in India. He said that "British investment in 1955 amounted to £300 million (Rs. 400 crores) which represented 82% of all foreign investments in India."

India's foreign long-term assets were primarily held by

the official sector with total holdings of Rs. 1,112 crores. The share of the private sector stood at Rs. 63 crores. The magnitude of business investments owned abroad was insignificant. The total long-term liabilities and assets owed to and owned in Britain and the international institutions, more or less, matched each other, the liabilities amounting respectively to Rs. 569 crores and Rs. 234 crores and the assets respectively to Rs. 558 crores and Rs. 229 crores. The liabilities to the U. S. A. stood at Rs. 125 crores while the assets held in that country amounted to Rs. 3 crores.

At the end of 1953, the overall position of the country, taking both long-term and short-term obligations in accounts showed a net excess of assets over liabilities of Rs. 500 crores. The surplus on short-term accounts was Rs. 346 crores and that on long-term accounts Rs. 154 crores. While the official sector had net assets abroad to the extent of Rs. 900 crores, the private sector had net liabilities to the tune of Rs. 399 crores.

The net assets position of the official sector was attributable to the ownership of Government securities, deposits and the 'residual' items in foreign countries. On the other hand, the private sector was a net debtor because of a large volume of foreign business investments. India had a net creditor position with Britain, Pakistan and Burma amounting respectively to Rs. 378 crores, Rs. 266 crores and Rs. 47 crores, and a net debtor position with the U. S. A. and the I. M. F. and I. B. R. D. amounting to Rs. 80 crores and Rs. 54 crores. India had an excess of assets over liabilities because of a substantial holding of British securities in Britain. On the other hand, the net creditor position with Pakistan and Burma was due to inter-Governmental debt payable by those countries to India. The net liabilities to the U. S. A. were accounted for mainly by the loan extended by the U. S. Government to India.

Compared to 1948, the country's total foreign liabilities showed an increase of Rs. 261 crores and the total foreign assets a fall of Rs. 542 crores. Over this period there was an aggregate change in the value of financial obligations—increase in foreign liabilities and reduction in foreign assets

—to the extent of Rs. 803 crores mainly on short-term account. The partition of the country had made India largely dependent on foreign sources for a part of its food and raw material requirements. Besides, the developmental needs of the country's economy had rendered necessary the import of capital equipment on a large-scale. Thus during the five years and a half ending 1953, the total import surplus amounted to Rs. 600 crores. The net reduction in foreign exchange reserves attributable to current transactions during this period was to the tune of Rs. 234 crores and would have been much higher but for the significant receipts of foreign official loans and the inflow of private foreign investments. With the conclusion of the Indo-U. S. negotiations for India's third wheat loan, which, like the second one, would amount to about 3.5 million tons, valued at Rs. 150 crores, the U. S. official and non-official economic assistance to India would amount in 1957 to about 1.300 million dollars (Rs. 6,500 million) since it started in 1952.[1]

The increased private foreign investment is claimed to have helped replace and expand the industrial and commercial structure in the country. The total net increase in our foreign business investment since 1948 was of the order of Rs. 132 crores, of which 80% belongs to the 'direct' investment category. Investment from Britain and the U. S. A. increased by Rs. 137 crores and Rs. 13 crores respectively, while investment from Pakistan and Ceylon declined by Rs. 7 crores and Rs. 2 crores respectively. Fresh investment from both Britain and the U. S. A. was predominantly of a 'controlled' variety, the percentage of controlled investment to the total increase being 85 for Britain and 91 for the U. S. A. Controlled investment is no other than investment of the 'direct' category, as distinguished from the 'portfolio' investment. Controlled investment, therefore, is investment accompanied by control from abroad over the policies of the companies concerned. While the flow of new capital from the U. S. A. was confined largely to the trading sector, that from Britain went to different sectors, such as manufacturing (Rs. 56

1. *The Statesman, July 8, 1957.*

8

crores), plantations (Rs. 21 crores), trading (Rs. 20 crores), utilities (Rs. 19 crores) and financial (Rs. 14 crores).[1] According to a statement made by India's then Finance Minister, Mr. Krishnamachari, in Lok Sabha on August 8, 1957, foreign firms remitted more than Rs. 27 crores as profits out of the country during 1956-57. Of this sum about Rs. 22 crores and 4 lakhs went to Britain.

A New Delhi report,[2] states that as the result of the recent Mission to India of Sir Norman Kipling, Director-General of the Federation of British Industries, British industrialists are likely to allow this country credit facilities amounting to Rs. 30 crores for the import of capital goods on deferred payments. This special fund would provide credit for Indian projects in which British firms might participate and repayments to the fund would be guaranteed by the Government of India. A Committee of Indian engineers presided over by Sir Jehangir Ghandy, to which the U. K. Mission's report as well as the report of a team of Soviet heavy machinery experts was referred, is said to have come to the conclusion that the British report should be accepted. It is, of course, suggested that for financial reasons and also on the ground of suitability the Ghandy Committee of experts have preferred the U. K. scheme to the Soviet offer. It is learnt that the Government of India are generally agreeable to the findings of the Committee, although they may be prepared to implement them by and through an integrated scheme embracing both the British and Soviet offers. A substantial portion of the credit thus offered by the U. K. will be used immediately to go ahead with the projects proposed by the U. K. Heavy Engineering Mission known as the Eric Coates Mission.

Let us now turn to India's foreign trade in particular. Of her Rs. 523.1 crores worth of export in 1953-54, Rs. 273.4 crores worth or 52.2% went to the Commonwealth countries, including Rs. 148.7 crores worth of exports to Britain. Of Rs. 573.9 crores worth of imports Rs. 278.9

1. *The figures and statements referred to in the text are reproduced from the Reserve Bank of India's survey of India's foreign liabilities and assets published from Bombay in 1955.* 2. *The Statesman, April 25, 1957*

crores worth or 48.7% came from the Commonwealth countries, including Rs. 142.7 crores worth of imports from Britain.[1] During the same period the export and import in respect of the Soviet Union and People's Democracies in Eastern Europe was valued at Rs. 1,15,19,901 and Rs. 59,70,907 respectively.[2] In 1955, 82% of India's total exports went to Britain, the U. S. A. and the Western European countries. The share of imports from these countries to India was 84%. During the same period the shares of India's export and import trade with the Soviet Union[3] and the Peoples' Democracies in Eastern Europe were 0.7% and 1.4% respectively.

The increase of Britain's share in India's foreign trade on the basis of percentage was as follows :

Year	Exports	Imports
1938-39	8%	9%
1949-50	25.7%	16.7%
1954-55	27.5%	25.4%

India's share in the world's shipping tonnage is only ·53%. She is entirely dependent on foreign shippers, mainly British, for her foreign trade. Until the end of the first five-year plan, India depended mainly on Britain for the supply of capital goods. That trend is still visible despite certain deals with the Soviet Union. Besides, one of India's most effective financial links with Britain is through the sterling balance reserves. Our currency is linked with the sterling for the purposes of foreign trade except where special agreements to the contrary are made.

Vulnerability of India's Position

All the facts stated above demonstrate the vulnerability of India's position in the world's picture, especially in relation to the United Kingdom. As a matter of fact, the

1. *The Eastern Economist, December 17, 1954*
2. *The Statesman, October 14, 1954*
3. In the course of an article published in *Hindusthan Standard* on Feb. 24, 1958 ; Mr. A. Akimov writes that the trade turnover between India and the U. S. S. R. in the period from January to November, 1956, reached Rs. 2.32 million thus surpassing more than four times the level of 1955. The turnover in 1955 was Rs. 55.2 million, whereas that for 1956 was Rs. 232.2 million. Of the latter figure the export claimed Rs. 97.1 million and the import Rs. 135.1 million.

India of today is a legacy of British rule and British economy extending over 200 years or more. The Indian defence force has been trained and built in the British military traditions. Its technique, tactics and strategy have been and are cast in the British mould. The latest instance of the Commonwealth defence collaboration is furnished by a 4-Day Commonwealth Naval Conference which opened in London on April 29, 1957. The main purpose of the Conference, as *Reuter* reports, was to enable the Commonwealth Chiefs of Naval Staff to "study matters of common interest in naval strategy and tactics in the light of current developments." *Reuter* adds that the Conference "will examine the implications of cold limited and global war for naval strategy and its central purpose will be to maintain the strong liaison between the Commonwealth navies."[1]

A far more revealing statement was made in the Lords on May 9, 1957, by Lord Home Secretary for Commonwealth Relations in the debate on the British Government's new five-year defence plans. These plans would concentrate, among other things, on nuclear weapons to prevent, it is claimed, an all-out war. For once after a long period, these plans were approved without a vote, the Lords Temporal and the Lords Spiritual, the Tory Lords and the Labour Lords all evidently making a common cause in the pursuit of peace, happiness and freedom ! The noble Lord said that the co-operation of the Commonwealth ran through all the Governments' defence plans. Canada was Britain's most intimate partner in the NATO. Australia and New Zealand were also partners in this great 'security' organisation. The latter two countries, further, were co-operating wholeheartedly on the ground in Malaya to save that accursed colony from the 'Communist bandits'. Pakistan, continued the Commonwealth Secretary, was a member both of the SEATO and the Bagdad Pact. An agreement had also been made recently with the Union of South Africa about the sea routes round the Cape, being some sort of a reserve strategic and economic opening in the event of the Suez failing ultimately to suit British

1. *The Statesman, April 30, 1957*

requirements in peace as well as in war. "All these regional organisations", observed the noble Lord, "have their military planning committees. The Commonwealth must be defended regionally on a regional basis today, and plans are being kept up both for global and limited war in these regional organisations."

Lest one should think that the Union of India, that is, Bharat had no place in this Grand Commonwealth Strategy and that the noble Lord and his Government were indifferent to Indian men, women and children in the face of the Communist menace from across the Himalayas and the Hindu Kush, the Commonwealth Secretary took the earliest opportunity to repel that insulting insinuation and stated: "Let it not be thought that because India and Ceylon do not accept regional military commitments, they do not have a very *close liaison* (italics ours) with our armed forces. On the contrary, we help them with *training and equipment* (italics ours).... The co-operation of the U. K. and the Commonwealth countries *is an absolute part* (italics ours) of our defence plans."[1]

Again, the Civil Service has been trained to follow British tradition and usage. The police is, by no means, an exception to this rule. The entire structure of the country's economy has been built on British practice. The company law, accounting and auditing and other trade, commercial and financial techniques are borrowed from the British. Indeed, there is the British stamp everywhere—in the hierarchy of administration, in the civil service and police, in the armed forces and military organisations, in the overall economy of the country and, above all, in the way of life as represented in the principles of British jurisprudence. In the leadership of the country there is, it seems, an overwhelming sense of dependability on all that is British despite New Delhi's nationalist chauvinism. There is neither initiative nor a keen awareness of our capacity, physical, mental and spiritual, to remake India and to recreate values in accordance with our needs and requirements, although one hears loud talks about reconstruction and the freedom of mind and spirit.

1. *The Statesman, May 11, 1957.*

Invisible Links

It is true that there is nothing in the legal relationship between India and Britain—no more, indeed, than in that between any Commonwealth State and Britain—that stands in the way of our seceding from the Commonwealth. Pandit Nehru says that while he has for the present decided to continue to remain within the Commonwealth, India may reconsider the position in the days ahead. That might be a threat, but one has reasons to suspect that it is an attempt to steal the thunder of the left. In the present set-up of things and in the context of the events that led to the transfer of power there is little or no possibility of India's breaking from the Commonwealth. The present leadership, who agreed to the partition of India in violation of their past pledges to prepare the ground for a compromise with the Muslim League and the British Government as a condition precedent to the transfer of power, must have persuaded themselves that to secede from the Commonwealth would expose themselves to great risks on the ideological and political planes and upset their apple-cart.

One of the strongest motives influencing the British decision to partition the Indian subcontinent was to play off Pakistan against India and *vice versa*, so that they could gain a position of strategic vantage and exploit both and create an atmosphere of mutual hatred and distrust between the two. With Pakistan within the Commonwealth and wedded to the SEATO and the Bagdad Pact India cannot and would not break away from the Commonwealth without a prior agreement or treaty with the U. S. A. or the U. S. S. R. To hobnob with the U. S. A. inevitably leads her to the SEATO and Bagdad while an agreement or treaty with the U. S. S. R. tends to make her dependent on an economy and the way of life which ultimately cannot but undermine, by the motion of its own law, the very basis of a bureaucracy-ridden plutocracy which is India today.

Or it may be there were certain secret treaties and agreements or understandings between the Indian leadership and the British Government providing the basis for those "invisible links" of which one has heard so much. And secret treaties and agreements, it is well-known, are part of diplomacy. It may be recalled in this connection that Lord Listowell, who had gone to Burma before the latter became independent, as the leader of a British Goodwill Mission, addressed a Press Conference on his return to London and said : "As the necessary corollary of the transference of power, a treaty was made with Burma the details of which I am not at liberty to divulge at present." And Burma is not far distant from India. As a matter of fact, in the House of Commons debate immediately after the Attlee Government's (Labour) declaration, 1947, solemnly promising to transfer power to India by June, 1948, Sir Stafford Cripps, a top-leader of that Government, took the opportunity to allay the misgivings of the Conservative Party and observed : "Proper protection of the minorities was made a condition of transfer, as was indeed the negotiating of a treaty as to the condition of transfer.... It will make provision for the protection of racial and religious minorities."[1]

So far as the Muslims, the biggest minority, were concerned, partition was subsequently offered to them and predominantly Muslim areas in India's north-western and eastern belts were constituted into an 'independent' Pakistani Dominion. At the time of Sir Stafford's speech one of the most important racial minorities was the British community engaged in industry, trade or business in India or employed under the Government. Evidently the treaty referred to by Cripps envisaged due, proper and effective protection for British subjects of the Crown in India. These people are no longer Indian citizens in terms of the Constitution of India and as such have ceased to be a minority under our municipal law. It is nevertheless clear from the provisions of the Constitution[2] that the British Government insisted upon, and the ruling party in India acquiesced in, guarantees as to the proper and effective protection of British interests.

1. *The Statesman, March 6, 1947.*
2. *Articles 14, 21, 22, 27, 31, 367* (3) *and the Constitution* (*Declaration as to Foreign States*) *Order, 1950.*

This view is further confirmed by a contemporaneous statement made by Prime Minister Attlee in reply to Churchill's attack on the Labour Government's offer to transfer power. Attlee said : "When he (Churchill) talks of India he seems to have forgotten the Cripps Mission—the declaration made by his own interim Government—and our declaration has gone no further than that."[1] It may be recalled that the Cripps Mission (1942) proposed, amongst other things, a treaty between the British Government and the proposed Constitution-making Body to cover all necessary matters arising out of the transfer of responsibility.[2] These matters had been earlier specifically mentioned by Prime Minister Churchill in these words :

> "In August 1940, a statement was made about the aims and policy which we are pursuing in India. This amounted in short to a promise that as soon as possible after the War, India should attain Dominion status in full freedom and equality with this country and the other Dominions under a Constitution to be framed by Indians by agreement amongst themselves and acceptable to the main elements in the Indian national life. This was, of course, subject to the fulfilment of our obligations for the protection of minorities, including the Depressed Classes, and our treaty obligations to the Indian States and to a settlement of certain lesser matters arising out of our long association with the fortunes of the Indian subcontinent."[3]

Three things are, therefore, clear. First, there is no foundation for the myth that the British Labour Government were responsible for bringing about a drastic change in the Indian political situation in opposition to the Conservative Party, for the fact is that the deed of transfer was an agreed document. Second, the deed marked no fundamental departure from the principles laid down by Churchill in 1942. Third, the policy laid down by Churchill's War

1. *The Statesman, December 21, 1946.*
2. *The British War Cabinet's Proposals (March-April, 1942), para C (II).*
3. *Churchill's statement in the Commons in March, 1942.*

Government has been followed, with Labour support, in the case of Ghana and, subject to certain reservations, of Malaya as well. There are indications that, with appropriate changes here and there, the British are going to pursue it elsewhere as part of their Commonwealth-cum-Empire strategem.

On June 9, 1955, speaking at a reception to celebrate the official birthday of Queen Elizabeth II, Mr. Harekrishna Mahatab, the then Governor of Bombay, observed: "The evolution of the Crown of the United Kingdom was a unique feature in history, which had no parallel anywhere...... There the Crown had not only divested itself of all authority in favour of the people, but had also become the symbol of unity of many nations for the common purposes of mutual defence and assistance." So for the common purposes of *mutual defence and assistance* India cannot and would not break away from the Commonwealth whatever platitudes politicians may indulge from time to time and whatever power the Republic may possess in law to secede from the Commonwealth.

India Pursuing an Independent Foreign Policy (?)

Certain recent events as well as India's acknowledged right to secede from the Commonwealth have led some people here and abroad to believe that despite India's Commonwealth membership the Government of India have been rapidly evolving an independent foreign policy of their own even, where necessary, to the extent of prejudicially affecting in particular the interests of Britain and generally those of the Western Powers. That independent policy has been described by Prime Minister Nehru as one of 'dynamic neutralism'—an expression mechanically adopted, it appears, by the 'right' and the 'left' alike in statements, speeches and in contemporaneous scholarly as well as polemic literature.

That India is not a British imperialist stooge in the accepted sense of the expression must be admitted, contrary to that senseless allegation repeatedly made sometime ago both in this country and outside without taking into consideration the pattern of Commonwealth relationship and its political, economic and strategic implications. As a matter of fact, in the post-war era specially, no Commonwealth State is a British servitor and the underlying principle of Commonwealth membership is one of interdependence, of collaboration. But to admit all this is not to accept the proposition that India has been following an independent foreign policy without regard to the interests of Britain, the Commonwealth and international capitalism.

As to the right of secession, there is, I insist, no room for confusion. That right was inherent in Dominion status. It is not a right which India and Pakistan have acquired for the first time in consequence of the transfer of power in 1947 or of the emergence of these States as Republics within the Commonwealth. It is a right which the British had long since kept reserved for the faithful and which the latter came to possess on the attainment of political 'majority'. As early as in 1920, Mr. Bonar Law, Leader of the House of Commons, made an important pronouncement in Parliament in the following terms :

> "There is not a man in this House. ... who would not admit that the connection of the Dominions with the Empire depends upon themselves. If the self-governing Dominions, Australia, Canada chose to-morrow to say 'We will no longer make a part of the British Empire', we would not try to force them. Dominion Home Rule means the right to decide their own destinies."[1]

Bonar Law, be it noted, was a die-hard Tory and no soap-box platform orator. Then after the Declaration of the Imperial Conference of 1926, particularly on the passing of the Statute of Westminster, 1931, it was agreed that the reference to Commonwealth-members as 'freely associated' carried with it the obvious implication that any member was free to get out of the 'association' at its will and by unilateral action. It was not merely an expression of a pious wish. For, in moving the Second Reading of the Burma Independence Bill in 1947, Prime Minister Attlee said :

> "In our view, nations have the right to decide on the nature of their own government. The British

1. The Commonwealth Relations Office List, 1951, p. 54.

Commonwealth of Nations is a free association of peoples, not a collection of subject nations. When, therefore, after due consideration, the elected representatives of the people of Burma, chose independence, it was, I believe, the duty of His Majesty's Government to take the necessary steps to implement their decision."[1]

Parliament enacted the Burma Independence Act, 1947, and it was declared, as has already been pointed out, that Burma would become an independent country, "neither forming part of His Majesty's dominions nor entitled to His Majesty's protection." A similar step was taken in the case of *Eire* in 1948. When that State repealed the External Relations Act, 1936, and declared its independence from the Commonwealth the British Parliament passed the Ireland Act, 1949, acknowledging that the Republic of Ireland had ceased to be "part of His Majesty's dominions," while providing at the same time that the Republic should not be regarded as a foreign country. The latter provision was inserted with a view to retaining for hundreds of Irish citizens engaged in business or trade or otherwise employed in Britain the rights and privileges flowing from the British Nationality Act, 1948. Thus it is clear that the right of secession recognised in the constitutional and political structure of the Commonwealth has nothing to do with the foreign policy of a Commonwealth State. Nor does the exercise of that right, in any particular case, as in the case of Burma, justify the contention that the country concerned has embarked upon an independent foreign policy, although it may create opportunities for development in that direction which Commonwealth membership may not, for obvious reasons, fully encourage or sustain,

While on the subject of foreign policy it is interesting to recall a statement made by Lenin which is pregnant with meaning and which may give food for thought to the 'left' defenders of the Government of India's foreign policy. In September, 1917, on the eve of the October Revolution Lenin wrote: "The one is intimately bound up with the other, home policy with foreign policy. The country cannot

1. The Commonwealth Relations Office List, 1951, p. 54

be made capable of self-defence without the supreme heroism of the people in carrying out great economic reforms boldly and resolutely. And it is impossible to arouse the heroism of the masses without breaking with imperialism... ."[1] A country's foreign policy is, in broad outline, a projection of its internal policy, and the internal policy has reference mainly to the country's economic strength and military potential both in human and material resources. It is wrong to think that while a country's internal economy and mililary tactics and strategy may not be fully independent, it can nevertheless pursue a consistently independent foreign policy. To be half in the right and half in the wrong, as the saying goes, is to be in the wrong. Some indication has been given in the previous pages as to our position in these spheres, as to our large-scale dependability on the Commonwealth, especially on Britain, for our military equipment and economic and financial resources.

Not Two Giants but Three

In interpreting our foreign policy the assumption is made that in the world of today there are two mighty giants—(1) on the other side of the Himalayas and the Hindu Kush the dialectically evolving Soviet Colossus and (2) across the Atlantic the idealistically predetermined Dollar Plutocracy—and that other nations, big or small, are generally in the one camp or in the other. But it is claimed that the Government of India, contrary to this general world trend, have consistently refused to allow themselves to yield either to the romantic gestures of the revolutionary Communist music or to the seductive embellishments of the American freedom lyrics. The assumption seems, however, to ignore another strong international force, and that force is represented by the Commonwealth. Alone and by herself Britain has, of course, ceased to be a comparable world power side by side with the Soviet Union and the U. S. A., but it is not for nothing that she has evolved, and is still evolving, an 'energy-impulse', a 'gravitational force', as the atomic scientists put it in the context of property

1. Lenin: *Selected Works*, Vol. II, p. 117

of the universe which is supposed to fill space. And the Commonwealth is a factor which one would do well to remember while examining our position, power and status in the world community.

To be sure, the U. S. A.'s increasing economic penetration into India's economy is fraught with momientous consequences politically as well as ideologically. One may, in this connection, refer to a simultaneous announcement at New Delhi and Washington made on January 16, 1958, of a $ 225 million U. S. loan to India. The U. S. Ambassador, Mr. Ellsworth Bunker, while commenting on the U. S. loan programme, expressed the hope that "the assistance would be helpful not only to India but to entire Asia as well." For this he gave two reasons. First, a strong and economically healthy India would be a vital stabilising influence for the whole of Asia. Second, India would be in a position to demonstrate that progress could be achieved in Asia by a free democratic society. In other words, the loan programme is intended to assist India in meeting the Communist challenge and to use this country, if possible, as a baston of defence of what is understood in the West as democracy as opposed to the alleged Communist totalitarianism.

Whether or not these objectives which the American Administration and monopolists may have in mind would be realised is a question to which history alone could give the answer. It is nevertheless clear that there is no substance in the contention that while Pakistan is entirely in the grip of the American dollar and bullet, India has been consistently pursuing an independent policy of her own under Mr Nehru's leadership and carrying bread and butter to every Indian home. Of course, there is a difference between the Pakistan approach and the Indian approach, but in view of Mr. Bunker's comments the difference is rather one of degree than of kind. Take, again, the speech made to the Indian Council of World Affairs by Mr. Cabot Lodge, the U. S. roving ambassador at New Delhi, on February 14, 1958. He said: "Disagreements make headlines, but it might surprise many people both in

India and the United States to realise how often in the U. N. our two countries have agreed. In the past five years India and the United States have voted the same way in 45 major roll-call votes in the U. N. Assembly.... Truly, the record of collaboration between us and India is already quite impressive. And it gives every promise of growing with the years."[1]

Now, with the latest U. S. offer the total American aid to India since Independence amounts to $ 1,275 million or more than Rs. 600 crores, of which over 90% is from Government sources. Excluding the amount envisaged in the present American offer, India's total foreign indebtedness to date amounts to Rs. 600 crores, on which the rate of interest varies from 2½% in the case of Soviet credits and U. S. wheat loan to 8% in the case of some private deals with West Germany. The World Bank's interest rate is 4⅓%.

Apparently there are no strings attached to the U. S. aid, but in economic and financial deals between unequals the freedom of the recepient country must, of necessity, be very much restricted, particularly when, as in India, private capital continues to play a dominant role in trade, industry and business, and to a large extent controls the relations of production. It should also be remembered that for the present, at any rate, American capital represents the capitalist spearhead directed against Socialism and that Britain is toeing the American line notwithstanding growing internal contradictions.

It is admitted that there are differences, even contradictions, among members of the Commonwealth, for instance, the differences between India and Pakistan or those between them both on one side and the Union of South Africa on the other, or, again, those between India and Britain. But there is an underlying core of unity of approach in all their actions, if not always in verbal reactions to events.

It would perhaps not be out of place to refer, in connection with the question as to the exact character of the Commonwealth structure, to one or two important recent documents. In his article on *Ten Years of Indian*

1. *The Statesman, February 16, 1958*

Independence broadcast by the office of the U. K. High Commissioner in India on August 16, 1957, Attlee wrote :

"The real dividing line in the world today is between those who respect the dignity of the individual and believe in freedom and democracy, and those who believe in sacrificing the individual to the State, in dictatorship and in the denial of freedom. Which way will Asia go ?

"Here is where India's role is of such supreme importance... . She stands out today as the champion in Asia of the freedom of the human spirit.

"Had either Britain or India failed in 1945, it may well have resulted in all Asia's falling under dictatorships, led away by the false professions of those who have shown by their actions that their national democracy is only a cloak for tyranny."

Again,

"India has been well served by the civil servants and soldiers trained under British rule. India has retained what was best in the tradition of the past. ...

"Of equal importance has been the forward-looking attitude which, instead of dwelling on past grievances, is directed to the future. Old friendships are remembered and new ones formed. There are ... more United Kingdom citizens in India than before, and more than 100,000 Indians in Britain."

The points sought to be brought home to us and all concerned by Attlee are :

(1) That the India policy pursued by the Churchill Government since 1940 and laid down in concrete form in 1942 has succeeded ;

(2) That had that policy leading, as it did, to the partition of the country and, on the basis thereof, the transfer of power failed to commend itself to acceptance by the Congress and the Muslim League India would have gone Communist ;

(3) That the Government of India under the Congress leadership have chosen Attlee's and, for the matter of that, Churchill's side of the 'dividing line'—the side, that is, of

freedom and democracy as against the side of the Communist dictatorship and denial of human freedom ;

(4) That forgetting the past and old grievances the Government of India are reverting to old friendships and forming new friendships and setting an example to new Asian or African States of how the old traditions should be preserved and the freedom of the human spirit fostered and cultivated ; and

(5) That the Commonwealth States, though socially and geographically apart, are united by 'ties of history and common ideals' and bound together by 'intangible links' which, in times of stress, have proved their strength.

The next document is an article by an expert on Commonwealth affairs broadcast, again, by the office of the U. K. High Commissioner in India. It was written against the background of the Commonwealth Prime Ministers' Conference held in India in June-July, 1957. The writer says :

> "The Commonwealth has no Central Government, defence force or judiciary and no rigid rules and commitments. Like the United Kingdom, it has no written Constitution, but all its members are united by a common sense of values and ideals, and all have certain constitutional features in common. In spite of the wide diversities of race and tradition, they all have a broadly similar pattern of legislative, executive or judicial institutions. ...
>
> "The Queen has ... , in the case of the countries accepting her as their monarch, a relationship with the individuals comprising each country and also a relationship with the nation as a collective entity. In the case of the two republics (India and Pakistan), she has only the latter relationship."

The writer does not forget to point out that all the Commonwealth States, except Ghana, but including the Federation of Rhodesia and Nyasaland, are contracting parties to the G. A. T. T. (The General Agreement on Tariffs and Trade), which is, more or less, a Commonwealth variant of the old system of Imperial preference. While admitting that all the Commonwealth States have the right to break away from the association or partnership he states that they do not think in terms of the exercise of that right. And why? Because if it were not a basic assumption, writes this British expert, that the Commonwealth is not only a voluntary and friendly but also a *lasting partnership*, long-term planning would be meaningless. For good and obvious reasons the writer, unlike some spokesmen of our 'go-ahead' parties or groups, has no illusion about India's planning.

While in Rome, as they say, you must behave as Romans. Inside the Commonwealth your planning—social, economic and military—must, of necessity, be Commonwealth-like. Thus we fight shy of Socialism and consign Marx, Engels and Lenin to the museum and the silvery notes about the socialistic pattern of society from New Delhi twinkle down upon the adoring Commonwealth earth. One is reminded here of Lenin's insistence on "the need constantly to express and expose among the broadest working masses of all countries, and particularly of the backward countries, the deception systematically practised by the imperialist powers, which, under the guise of politically independent States, set up States that are wholly dependent upon them economically, financially and militarily."[1] How prophetic in the context of post-war developments in Asia and Africa!

It is interesting to recall an after-prayer speech at Delhi in June, 1947, made by Gandhiji in which he expressed the view that the "Congress Government in the Centre will inherit the international and internal obligations of the Government today."[2] This means, for example, that the previous British Government's commitment regarding Goa binds its successor—the present Government of India. All that finds support in the *communique* issued at the end of the Prime Ministers' Conference held in London in October, 1948. It stated that "the discussions have covered many matters of common concern, including international relations,

1. Lenin: *The National-Liberation Movement in the East*, p. 255
2. *The Statesman, June 9, 1947*

economic affairs and defence." The discussions, according to the *communique*, "had shown a substantial community of outlook among all the Commonwealth Governments in their approach to present world problems." The Commonwealth Governments resolved to work together "to establish world peace on a democratic basis." A general desire was expressed to "maintain and extend methods of consultation between members of the Commonwealth."[1]

It was followed by a meeting at the ministerial level held at Colombo in January, 1950, at the Ceylon Prime Minister's invitation. Asia was considered at the meeting to be both "the main focus of interest and the area of special urgency." It was noted with satisfaction that "there is a consistent identity of approach among all members of the Commonwealth on the fundamental issues underlying the current problems of foreign policy." It also noted with satisfaction "the political settlement reached in Indonesia and paid special attention to Indo-China, Burma, and Malaya." As regards Western Europe, the representatives of the other Commonwealth Governments took the view that there was "no inconsistency between the policy followed by the United Kingdom and the maintenance of traditional links between the United Kingdom and the rest of the Commonwealth."[2]

Speaking on the foreign affairs debate in the Commons on February 19, 1958, on his return from the Commonwealth tour Mr. Macmillan, Britain's Prime Minister, observed *inter alia* : "In this great world issue.........India—and the same is true of Pakistan and Ceylon—stands with us against Communist philosophy, for it is based upon a material view of life which is totally abhorrent to these people who, above all, cling to the spiritual foundation of their lives.... There were, of course, differences, even big differences, of emphasis and approach. The Indian Government and the Ceylonese, for instance, were against the various military groupings. Pakistan was not.... These are what I would call really tactical differences. The strategic object of all the Commonwealth countries is the

1. The Commonwealth Relations Office List, 1951, p. 65
2. *Ibid*, pp. 66-67

same—to maintain peace, to build up the prosperity of the whole upon a basis of individual freedom and parliamentary government and not on the basis of totalitarian control."[1]

All the documents and facts cited above show very clearly that, subject to occasional differences and even conflicts, members of the Commonwealth are basically united in their general approach to international problems, including the questions of war and peace, economic collaboration and military strategy. They show, that is, that there is, in the view of the Governments of the Commonwealth States, nothing in *Panch Shila*, including the principles of equality, respect for sovereignty, non-interference, non-aggression and peaceful co-existence and the Bandung spirit, which is repugnant to the Commonwealth idea and the Commonwealth partnership. They show, further, that there is no inconsistency between the latter and the overall strategy of the SEATO, NATO, and the Baghdad Pact. If some members of the Commonwealth are outside these Pacts and Agreements, as there are, it does not mean that they are no participants in the overall Commonwealth strategy. It seems that they represent its ideological sector, whereas the others are assigned the task of looking after the strategy's operational part. There is thus a division of functions and responsibilities among the members.

The USSR's Contributions to Peaceful Co-existence

The impression seems to have gained ground in certain quarters that the principles underlying *Panch Shila* and agreed to in treaties or agreements between India and the Peoples' Republic of China or between India and the U. S. S. R. constitute a departure from the fundamental Marxian doctrine as well as from the so-called Stalinist tradition. It has been suggested that the great Russian thaw, which has, since Stalin's passing in 1953, broken the alleged Communist ice age, has also released forces which had hitherto been suppressed by the Kremlin's iron rule under the dictatorship of a single person. It has further been claimed, though not officially in positive terms,

1. *Hindusthan Standard, February 21, 1958*

that Prime Minister Nehru's foreign policy is basically different from the Commonwealth policy and that apart from its effective peace offensive directed against the Anglo-American war-mongers it has succeeded in persuading both the Peking and Kremlin leaders to accept, for the first time in history, a new revolutionary mode of action in international relations, namely, the principle of peaceful co-existence. Marx, one is asked to believe, is now a museum curiosity, Lenin a played-out song and Stalin a total ideological wreckage. Gandhism fills the space and has become stricken humanity's article of faith and Nehru its recognised wholesale dealer. All this, it is needless to point out, is self-deception, and is evidence of infantile romanticism or of crude mental aberrations. There is, of course, no disputing the fact that Prime Minister Nehru is anti-war and that, I submit, is all. And what statesman of eminence in the world is today professedly pro-war ?

So far as peaceful co-existence is concerned, the idea should be historically examined from the two opposing points of view—that of the capitalist States and that of the Soviet Union. The success of the October Revolution and the emergence of a Soviet State in 1917, as history shows, had caused alarm in influential circles of the capitalist States and provoked their hostility. As many as fourteen States, including Germany, Britain, the U. S. A. and Japan launched a fierce attack upon this infant revolutionary State. Its territory was invaded and its ports bombarded. The colossal nature of the havoc wrought may be gathered from the fact that, in addition to Russia's four million dead between 1914 and 1917, she lost nearly one and a half million as a result of the armed intervention. To all this must be added destruction of railways, factories and mines. But the revolutionary Soviet State and its people refused to yield. It drove out the foreign invaders from its European territories in 1920, and from its Asian territories in 1922. Intervention had been successfully tried to smother the French Revolution, but this time in Russia the interventionists counted without their host. It is thus clear that by tradition and ideology some capitalist States, especially those that had big colonial empires, had been opposed, both in principle and in practice, to what has now come to be known in international relations as the principle of peaceful co-existence.

Look at the other side. Attention may be invited in this connection to an interesting letter addressed by Engels to Kautsky on September 12, 1882. In the course of that letter Engels wrote : "The victorious proletariat can force no blessings of any kind upon any foreign nation without undermining its own victory by so doing. Which, of course, by no means excludes defensive wars of various kinds." Surely, it is not Gandhism in the sense that the only effective antidote to violence is non-violence, but at the same time there is nothing in Engels' proposition that may be interpreted as encouraging or supporting intervention by a Socialist State in the internal arrangements of a foreign State for the purpose of grafting a revolution. It envisages, on the other hand, the possibility, in certain circumstances, of a Socialist State living side by side with bourgeois or even feudal States. I need not pursue this matter by citing extracts from the numerous speeches and writings by Lenin in support of this proposition, for it is not Lenin so much as Stalin who has come in for denunciation during the last three or four years as having consistently sponsored and carried out a policy of hostility to the world's capitalist States. To Stalin and his precept and practice I should now turn.

Stalin on Peaceful Co-existence

Students of history are well aware of the famous struggle between Stalin and Trotsky on the question of 'Socialism within a country' *versus* 'a world revolution,' of the conflict between those who, having captured power, would rest content with building Socialism within the boundaries of the revolutionary State and those who saw no future for Socialism unless the Socialist or Bolshevik revolution was carried across the borders and the stage set for a revolutionary show-down on a world scale. They are familiar with the oft-quoted Stalinist maxim that revolution cannot be carried in a leather suit-case beyond the frontiers. Ultimately Stalin won in this struggle. Let us see how Joseph E. Davies, the U. S. A. Ambassador to the Soviet Union during 1936-39, reacted to the contemporaneous events. He wrote : "Lenin suffered stroke in 1922 and died in 1924. ... By 1924 the Central Government had managed to balance its budget... . The Trotsky wing was advocating world revolution, whereas the Stalin-followers were advocating the projection of the Communistic principle in the Soviet Union first."[1] In a different context Davies observed : "Stalin, historically, will be recognised as the great builder in Russia, following Peter the Great."[2]

Davies was a seasoned bourgeois statesman and a lawyer to boot. He was no Communist, not even a fellow-traveller. He had no partiality for the Soviet Union, for Stalin or for Marxism as such. By no test or standard can the opinion expressed by such an eminent authority be dismissed as being of no weight or importance. What Davies wrote in 1938 has been fully and with greater warmth endorsed by Anna Louise Strong, a famous writer on problems relating to the Soviet Union, its leadership and its people. She says : "On one thing, they will not differ. As far as any individual may claim the events he led, Lenin made the Russian Revolution, Stalin built the world's first Socialist country... ."[3]

In September 1927, replying to an American Labour delegation Stalin said : "I think that the existence of two opposite systems, the capitalist system and the Socialist system, does not exclude the possibility of agreements. I think that such agreements are possible and expedient in conditions of peaceful development. Exports and imports are the most suitable ground for such agreements... . The same thing may be said in regard to the diplomatic field. We are pursuing a policy of peace, and we are prepared to sign a pact of non-aggression with bourgeois States. We are pursuing a policy of peace, and we are prepared to come to an agreement concerning disarmanent, including complete abolition of standing armies, which we declared to the whole

1. Joseph E. Davies : *Mission to Moscow*, p. 250
2. *Ibid*, p. 197
3. Anna Louise Strong : *The Stalin Era*, p. 126

world as far back as the time of the Genoa Conference.[1] Here is a basis for agreement in the diplomatic field. ... "[2]

At the 15th Congress of the C. P. S. U. in December, 1927, Stalin declared : "The maintenance of peaceful relations with the capitalist countries is an obligatory task for us. Our relations with the capitalist countries are based on the assumption that the co-existence of two opposite systems is possible. Practice has fully confirmed this."[3]

Again, at the 18th Congress of the C. P. S. U. in March, 1939, Stalin reiterated the Soviet policy of peaceful co-existence and observed : "We stand for peace and the strengthening of business relations with all countries. That is our position, and we shall adhere to this position, so long as these countries maintain like relations with the Soviet Union, and so long as they make no attempt to trespass on the interests of our country."[4] Writing to the Secretary of State on May 10, 1939, Joseph E. Davies, the U. S. A. Ambassador to the Soviet Union, observed : "... the Soviet position is definitely devoted to peace, both because of ideological and economic reasons."[5]

Earlier, that is, in November, 1930, Mr. Walter Duranty, a well-known American journalist, asked Stalin if he thought it possible or desirable that the capitalist and Communist systems should exist side by side without fighting. Stalin's reply was as simple as it was unhesitating. He said : "They have not fought for ten years, which means they can co-exist. We don't want to fight and some of their people don't either."[6]

Lest there should be any misconception about Stalin's post-war role in the matter of peaceful co-existence it is worth while referring to his replies to questions put to him in September, 1946, by Alexander Werth, Moscow correspondent of the *Sunday Times*, in the context of a speech made by Henry Wallace urging closer and friendlier relations

1. The Conference was held in April, 1922
2. Andrew Rothstein : *Peaceful Co-existence*, p. 39
3. *Ibid*, p. 40
4. *Ibid*, p. 41
5. Joseph E. Davies : *Mission to Moscow*, p. 283
6. Andrew Rothstein : *Peaceful Co-existence*, p. 43

between the U.S.A. and the U.S.S.R. In the course of his replies Stalin asserted (i) that he believed in the possibility of friendly and lasting co-operation between the Soviet Union and the Western Democracies and friendly competition between the two systems despite ideological differences ; (ii) that the strengthening of political, commercial and cultural ties would considerably contribute to the establishment of such friendly relations ; (iii) that with the progress of the Soviet Union towards Communism the possibilities of its peaceful co-operation with the outside world would grow rather than decrease ; and (iv) that 'Communism in one country' was perfectly possible, especially in a country like the Soviet Union.[1]

Like sentiments were expressed by Stalin in his reply to Elliot Roosevelt in December, 1946, and also in his reactions in May, 1948, to Henry Wallace's proposals for a settlement of American-Soviet differences. He assured Wallace that notwithstanding the differences in economic systems and ideologies "the co-existence of these systems and the peaceful settlement of differences between the U.S.S.R. and the U.S.A. are not only possible but absolutely necessary in the interests of the universal peace."[2] In April, 1952, fifty American editors put to Stalin the question : "On what basis is the co-existence of capitalism and Communism possible ?" To that Stalin's reply was : "The peaceful co-existence of capitalism and Communism is fully possible given the mutual desire to co-operate, readiness to perform obligations which have been assumed, observance of the principle of equality and non-interference in the internal affairs of other States." It was published in April, 1952. Here then you find Stalin foreshadowing those basic principles in inter-State relations which, four years later, passed current as *Panch Shila* under an ancient Indian name.[3]

1. Andrew Rothstein : *Peaceful Co-existence*, pp 48-49 2. *Ibid*, p. 49

3. More than 2,500 years ago Gautama Buddha had given stricken humanity this now-famous slogan as a rule of conduct for individuals in their mutual relations. The principles enunciated by the Buddha were : (i) abstain from destroying life ; (ii) abstain from speaking falsehood ; (iii) abstain from taking what has not been given unto thee ; (iv) abstain from false behaviour in matters of love ; and (v) abstain from intoxicants.

The Soviet Union's interest in the preservation of peace has been and is genuine, having regard to the terrible losses incurred since the Revolution in 1917, especially during World War II. Seven million Soviet citizens lost their lives and one-third of the national wealth was destroyed. Its loss was greater than that of Britain and the U.S.A. or that of Germany. The Soviet citizens have experienced the horrors of a modern total war as no other people perhaps have in history, ancient, mediaeval or modern. There is not a single family in that country that has not lost one or more of its near and dear ones in war. It was, therefore, necessary for the Union to restore the afflicted areas, develop industry and agriculture, surpass the West in industrial and agricultural output, raise the standard of living of the working people and give them a sense of security. Its peace-loving policy is dictated by its own interests and in the Socialist cause.

While conceding that theoretically the contradictions between capitalism and Socialism are stronger than the contradictions among the capitalist countries themselves Stalin, it may be recalled, expressed his doubt about the possibility of the capitalist States precipitating a war with the Soviet Union. He assigned two reasons for his view. First, because war with the Soviet Union, as a Socialist land, was more dangerous to capitalism than war between capitalist countries themselves. For, whereas war between capitalist countries might raise the question of supremacy of certain capitalist countries over others, war with the Soviet Union was likely to put capitalism out of 'action. Second, the capitalist States themselves did not believe, notwithstanding propaganda to the contrary, that the Soviet Union had any aggressive intentions because they were aware of its peaceful policy, because they knew that it would not itself attack them.[1]

Stalin thought that the disintegration of the single, all-embracing world market was "the most important sequel of the Second World War and of its economic consequences."

---

1. J. Stalin: *Economic Problems of Socialism in the U. S. S. R.* (1952), p. 39

It had, according to him, deepened "the general crisis of the capitalist system."[1] Naturally, the sphere of exploitation of the world's resources by the major capitalist countries (U.S.A., Britain and France) would, in his opinion, contract rather than expand. This phenomenon was interpreted by him as having revealed, in broad outline, the deepening of the general crisis of the world capitalist system in connection with the disintegration of the world market. From these points of view Stalin stated that Lenin's famous thesis that "imperialism inevitably generates war" was not obsolete, that the inevitability of *wars between capitalist countries* remained in force, despite the fact that powerful popular forces had come forward in defence of peace and against another world war.[2] It is, therefore, wrong to suggest, as has been suggested in certain circles, that Stalin spoke of the inevitability of wars between the Soviet Union and capitalist States. All that he said was that so long as imperialism was there, wars were inevitable but not necessarily between Socialist States and capitalist States but between capitalist States themselves.

Khrushchov and Bulganin on Stalin

In the light of the proceedings of the 20th Congress of the C. P. S. U. held in 1956, and the varied reactions they have produced all the world over it is interesting to refer to the observations made by Khrushchov and Bulganin in their respective reports to the 19th Congress, that took place in 1952, on the correctness or otherwise of Stalin's theoretical contributions and his leadership of the Soviet State. Khrushchov stated amongst other things :

> "A new and inestimable contribution to the Marxist-Leninist theory is Comrade Stalin's *Economic Problems of Socialism in the U. S. S. R.* In this work, creatively developing the science of Marxism-Leninism, he arms the Party and the Soviet people with the theory of the economic laws of modern capitalism and of Socialism,

1. J. Stalin : *Economic Problems of Socialism in the U.S.S.R.* (1952), p. 34
2. *Ibid*, pp. 40-41

and of the preliminary condition for the transition from Socialism to Communism."[1]

Again,

"Comrade Stalin's work on economic problems, like his other writings, is of immense value in the solving of the problems connected with the building of a Communist society and in educating party members and all the working people in the immortal ideas of Leninism."[2]

Furthermore,

"Comrade Stalin teaches us that after a correct line has been laid down, after the correct solution of a problem has been indicated, success depends upon organisational work, upon the organisation of the effort to carry the party line into effect."[3]

In his speech to the Congress Bulganin observed :

"*In the Economic Problems of Socialism in the U. S. S. R.*, the new outstanding work of Comrade Stalin, he points out that in preparation for this transition (from Socialism to Communism) an uninterrupted expansion of all social production must be assured, with a relatively higher rate of expansion in the production of means of production, and that by means of gradual transitions collective-farm property must be raised to the level of public property, that commodity circulation must be superseded, also by means of gradual transitions, by a system of products-exchange, and that finally such a cultural advancement of society must be attained as will ensure the all-round development of manual and mental abilities of every member of society .... The programme of our country's development mapped out by the draft directions takes precisely the course indicated by Stalin... ."[4]

Continuing Bulganin quotes with approval the analysis of the present situation in the capitalist world made by Stalin to the effect :

1. Khrushchov's *Report on the Amendments to the Rules of the C. P. S. U.*, p. 8
2. *Ibid*, p. 8 3. *Ibid*, p. 6 4. Bulganin's *Speech to the Congress*, p. 18

"Outwardly, everything would seem to be 'going well': The U. S. A. has put Western Europe, Japan and other capitalist countries on rations; Germany (Western), Britain, France, Italy and Japan have fallen into the clutches of the U. S. A., and are meekly obeying its commands. But it would be mistaken to think that things can continue to 'go well' for 'all eternity', that these countries will tolerate the domination and oppression of the United States endlessly, that they will not endeavour to tear loose from American bondage and take the path of independent development."[1]

Again,

"Our Party has come to its Nineteenth Congress united, firmly cemented around its Leninist-Stalinist Central Committee, around Comrade Stalin."[2]

Of special significance is Bulganin's assessment of Stalin's policy in war and peace. Said Bulganin :

"Before the war and since our people have applied their efforts chiefly to peaceful construction. The Soviet Union prosecuted a firm and consistent foreign policy of peace. At the same time our Party was never oblivious of the threat of war, of imperialist machinations, and, under Stalin's wise leadership, has put the country and army in readiness for active defence."[3]

Furthermore,

"The utterances of the Party, of the great Stalin, armed the Soviet people with an extraordinarily effective weapon—profound faith in the triumph of our just cause. Recall, Comrades, the stern days of the autumn of 1941 when the Hitlerities were pressing on Moscow, the capital of our country. The foe was jubilant and was already making preparations to celebrate the victory. The clique across the ocean that is now preparing a new war likewise looked forward to the early demise of Soviet rule.

"And it was during these crucial days that Comrade Stalin delivered his two addresses, one on November 6

1. Bulganin's *Speech to the Congress*, p. 24 2. *Ibid*, p. 24 3. *Ibid*, pp. 5-6

devoted to the 24th anniversary of the Great October Revolution, and the other the next day at the Red Army Parade, from the rostrum of the Lenin mausoleum.... .

"The heartening effect of Comrade Stalin's utterances can hardly be overestimated. They shed brilliant light upon the course which our struggle would take, raised the spirits of our people and troops, cheered up all the friends of the Soviet Union abroad and caused alarm in the camp of the enemy.

"Everything turned out exactly the way Comrade Stalin had said it would. The Soviet Army not only cleared its native land of the enemy but also carried out its great mission of liberation."[1]

Again,

"Each one of these victories is a concrete embodiment of the Soviet art of war, of the skill of Soviet officers and generals, is a triumph of the Stalin military science, a triumph of the generalship of our leader and Supreme Commander-in-Chief, Comrade Stalin.

"Comrade Stalin headed the fight of the Soviet people and of our Armed Forces against foreign invasion. It was under his direct leadership and in accordance with the plans designed by his genius that all decisive operations in the Great Patriotic War were prepared and carried into execution and that the defeat of Hitler Germany and imperialist Japan became a reality."[2]

The opinions expressed by these two eminent Soviet leaders in the above-quoted passages lend support to Stalin's formulations on the economic laws of modern capitalism and Socialism, emphasise Stalin's contributions in creatively developing Marxism-Leninism and endorse Stalin's thesis about the deepening of capitalist crisis and unavoidable conflicts, sooner or later, between or among the capitalist States. They also prove that while Stalin laboured successfully to put the country and army in readiness for active defence, he prosecuted a firm and consistent foreign policy of peace. They are, further, a clear and emphatic admission

1. Bulganin's *Speech to the Congress*, pp. 9-10 2. *Ibid*, p. 13

that Stalin played a heroic role in the conduct of World War II, and by his wise guidance, brought victory to the Soviet Union and liberation to the Eastern European States.

If the sentiments expressed in these authoritative documents were genuine, one can only say that the *New York Times* report of Khrushchov's alleged speech to a secret session of the 20th Congress denouncing Stalin was a complete fabrication. For, one hates to believe that the Soviet leaders of the eminence of Khrushchov and Bulganin would profess sentiments in which they did not at all believe merely because they had been terrified by the presence of Stalin. Even if they had not had the courage to face him openly and speak out their minds, they could at least have refrained from making such laudatory remarks about a man whom one of them, as alleged, felt constrained, only four years later, to attack so savagely. Incidentally, it must be noted that Khrushchov has since contradicted the report and stated that Stalin was a great Marxist and that in their approach towards the capitalist States they were all Stalinists.

Nobody denies that 1956 was not 1952, that Stalin dead and lying inert in the Lenin mausoleum was not equal to Stalin alive and kicking. But already by 1952, the Communists had captured power in Eastern European States and China and nothing happened during the last four years which challenged, in theory or in practice, the fundamentals of Marxism, the basic tenets of Leninism and the formulations of Stalin by way of contributions to creative Marxism-Leninism.

Peaceful Co-existence no Actionless Drama

There must be no confusion as to the implications of the five principles of peaceful co-existence and, for that matter, of the principles rendered famous in history as *Panch Shila.* Co-existence does not mean abandonment by the classes concerned of their respective ideologies. Co-existence is by no means an admission that the economic laws of capitalism or the economic laws of Socialism or the laws of development of society have become obsolete because Karl Marx told his fascinating story of mankind about a century ago or because Gautama Buddha waged his heroic battle against fanatical Brahminical orthodoxy more than two thousand and five hundred years ago or because Jesus of Nazareth preached his sermons on the Mount about two thousand years ago. The world is doubtless changing but it is changing within the limitations of what may be called physical realism and subject to the basic patterns of social development. Co-existence does not rule out moral or material support being given to oppressed peoples struggling for freedom and independence or to undeveloped or underdeveloped countries fighting against poverty, disease and squalor and seeking to raise the standard of living of men and women toiling in factory and field.

Peaceful co-existence implies healthy competitive existence, so that in the course of such existence that system will prevail which is the best. Peaceful co-existence repudiates the doctrine of bolstering up or destroying a system by brute force applied across the frontiers of a State. Co-existence, however, does not, in theory or in practice, eliminate the possibility of the application of a stronger social force to overcome the armed resistance of the obsolescent forces of society where the basic economic law that the relations of production must necessarily conform to the character of the productive forces is sought to be retarded by violent methods or organised terror. Peaceful co-existence is not mechanical acceptance of the *status quo*, a plea for an insipid, actionless drama of life or a full-stop to the liberating urges of mankind. Peaceful co-existence is a rule of conduct for States in their mutual relations and has no application whatsoever to the ideological struggles of mutually hostile economic classes or to proletarian co-operation on an international scale.

The fact, however, is that those difficult and anxious years in which Socialism was built within one country, as in the Soviet Union, that is, from 1917 to the end of World War II are, in a significant way, ended, for no longer do we speak, with the famous Red Dean, of the Socialist Sixth. Socialism is today the philosophy, yes, the mode of action on one-third of the earth's surface, and surely this has changed certain aspects of the problem of mankind. But yet the core of the problem remains : the mass hunger set against the scarcity economy : the urge of a better and nobler life set against the resistance of the obsolescent forces of society ; the passion for freedom set against the slavery imposed by an exploiting minority ; the struggle for national self-determination set against colonial domination ; and, in short, the dynamics of revolution set against the safety devices of counter-revolution or reformism.

By or through its friendship with what is known as the neutral bloc the Socialist one-third may align itself with another one-third of the earth's population in a common anti-war front and isolate the war-mongers. From that point of view the Leninist thesis about 'the inevitability of wars' seems to have undergone revision at the hands of the Kremlin's present collective leadership. But yet the problem remains : Can this post-war phenomenon eliminate civil wars or localised wars or eventually wars between capitalist States ? Can it facilitate the peaceful liquidation of capitalism or imperialism ? Can it change the basic character of the Commonwealth, which is neither anti-colonial nor anti-capitalist but is by tradition, antecedents and social pattern definitely hostile to scientific Socialism ? All the indications are that possibly it cannot.

Nor should, in this context, exaggerated importance be attached to Mr. Nehru's denunciation of the Eden misadventure over the Suez in 1956, for that little piece of angry but panicky muddle-headness on the part of Britain's Prime Minister came in for no less violent attack by the Eisenhower Administration, the British Labour Party and even a certain group of the Conservatives themselves. It was, in no sense, a conflict between the Governments of India and Britain ; it was, at the worst, a case of acute difference of opinion between the Government of India and the dominant section of Britain's ruling party headed by Eden. And in this the Government of India had the backing of the United States and the British Labour Party. Whatever the nature of the conflict, it has not in any way affected India's relationship with the Commonwealth which is cemented by ties that are easily explained but not so easily severed. Like matter, the Commonwealth seems to be the depository of strength. Like matter, again, the Commonwealth may change its forms or its colours, but its strength remains, its substance persists, and its 'radiation' or 'energy-impulse' is a constant quantity !

INDEX

C

D

E

F

G

H

I

J

K

L

M

N

S

T

U

W

Y

Z